Wri...

Awaken the Writer Within

Discover how to release your creativity and find your true writer's voice

CATHY BIRCH
2nd edition

How To Books

Published by How To Books Ltd,
3 Newtec Place, Magdalen Road,
Oxford OX4 1RE, United Kingdom.
Tel: (01865) 793806. Fax: (01865) 248780.
email: info@howtobooks.co.uk
http://www.howtobooks.co.uk

First edition 1998
Second edition 2001

British Library Cataloguing in Publication Data.
A catalogue record for this book is available from
the British Library.

Cartoons by Mike Flanagan
Cover design by Shireen Nathoo Design
Cover image by PhotoDisc

Produced for How To Books by Deer Park Productions
Typeset by Kestrel Data, Exeter
Printed and bound by Cromwell Press Ltd, Trowbridge, Wiltshire

NOTE: The material contained in this book is set out in good
faith for general guidance and no liability can be accepted
for loss or expense incurred as a result of relying in particular
circumstances on statements made in the book. Laws and
regulations are complex and liable to change, and readers should
check the current position with the relevant authorities before
making personal arrangements.

Contents

List of Illustrations

Preface

'The main struggle people have with creativity is that they stop themselves from doing what comes naturally.'
(Clarissa Pinkola Estés: *The Creative Fire*)

What were your favourite creative pastimes as a child? Did you sing and dance, paint, cook, make models, dress up and act out stories with your friends? Close your eyes for a moment and remember how it felt to do your favourite things for sheer enjoyment, with no anxieties about being 'good enough'. Remember how your creativity flowed.

If writing is one of your favourite things and, in doing it, you wish to recapture that sense of spontaneity and fun you had in childhood – this is the book for you. Its wide variety of exercises and visualisation techniques will enable you to explore the treasures of your subconscious, revisit your childhood world of games and make-believe and bring back what you find. Its practical advice will enable you to share these experiences with others through your work.

It also suggests ways of using time, space and equipment creatively, and of taking care of your health in ways specifically aimed at writers and the work they do. By combining the practical with the imaginative in this way, it will help you at every stage of the writing process. Its aim is to get you writing, keep you writing, and enable you to enjoy your work to the full.

Use this book to rediscover your love of words, find your voice and become the writer you were meant to be. Above all – have fun!

Cathy Birch

1

Writing – a Way of Life

This book is designed to stimulate and sustain your creative flow. It will help you through those difficult patches when inspiration seems to have deserted you, and the whole process feels like horribly hard work. It will help you celebrate and utilise to the full those exciting times when your creativity seems to take on a life of its own and you feel as though you are running to keep up with it. It will enable you to tap into that inner wealth you may have forgotten you had. If you can just remember to have this book to hand and turn to it when needed, you need never be stuck again.

This chapter looks at how our work habits might be improved in order to free that natural flow. Management of health, time, and resources is considered as part of this process. If you feel tempted to skip this in order to get down to writing straight away, then remember to return to it later. Many writers have found that the practical advice given here has solved some long-standing problems.

WRITING IS A PHYSICAL ACTIVITY

A writer is like an athlete; a 'competitor or skilled performer in physical exercises', to quote the *Concise Oxford Dictionary*. Because we spend so many hours sitting at our desks, it is easy to forget this – until our body protests. Our neck, shoulders and head ache, our eyes refuse to focus, our wrists succumb to repetitive strain syndrome, and then we remember that our mind operates through a physical organ in a physical body with needs of its own.

These aspects of a writer's physical make-up need particular attention:

- the brain
- the eyes

- digestion

- joints, muscles, heart and lungs.

Keep your brain alert

Like all our bodily organs our brain needs nourishment, a rich blood supply, plenty of oxygen and adequate rest in order to function well. Hours of sitting hunched in a stuffy room, skipping meals or eating junk food will put it at a disadvantage.

The simple acts of opening the window, circling your arms and breathing deeply will boost mental processes tremendously. If you find it hard to remember to do these things, write a note to yourself and place it where it will catch your eye from time to time.

Brain food

Our brains thrive on foods rich in iron, phosphorous and the B vitamins (particularly B6, which is said to help with 'writer's block'). Liver, fish, pulses, grains, wholemeal bread and green vegetables are all excellent writers' foods. My current favourite 'boost' is extract of malt. What's yours?

Brain fatigue

We need rest, not only to combat tiredness but to enable the body to replenish its cells. For this reason, burning the midnight oil – a common symptom of 'writing fever', may reduce our mental and physical efficiency over time. Many writers have found it beneficial to replace this habit with an early morning start when the world is quiet and the brain is rested.

Efficiency is also improved by a regular change of task – on average, every 1½ hours. (See Glossary: 'Circadian rhythms'). Use a timer with an audible signal as a reminder to take regular breaks.

Ideally, leave the work room and do something physical. Have a list of suggested activities to hand – anything from household tasks to a brisk walk around the block. Physical movement will invigorate your body. Also, it often triggers a flow of words and ideas (see 'Use physical activity to stimulate your creativity' below).

Brain waves

Your list could include some of the audio-visual products which use pulses of light and/or sound to alter brainwave patterns. A

15-minute session with one of these can calm an agitated brain, or revitalise a flagging one.

Highly recommended are the products available from *LifeTools* and the very reasonably priced *DeltaBeta* glasses from *Rontronics* (see Useful Addresses). **NB Pulsing lights should not be used by people suffering from epilepsy**.

Further suggestions for activity breaks appear in the sections which follow.

Checklist

To function well your brain needs:

- nourishment

- oxygen

- rest

- a well-exercised body

- regular breaks.

Keeping your eyes healthy

Computer users
If you use a word-processor, you probably spend many hours staring at the screen. An anti-glare screen, either built in or added on, is essential.

If over-exposure causes sore or itchy eyes, try bathing them with a cooled herbal infusion of eye-bright and camomile. (Also see 'All writers' below.)

Such exposure can leave eyes deficient in Vitamins A and B2, so supplements are advisable. Vitamins C and E also promote eye health.

Alleviate eye and neck strain by having the monitor exactly at eye-level. If necessary, place some blocks underneath it to achieve this.

All writers
Most methods of getting words onto paper involve your eyes in long periods of repetitive activity. They will function better if you take regular time out to exercise them. Add this 'eye-gymnastics' routine to your activities list:

- Hold an upright pencil about 10 cms from the bridge of your nose. Focus on something distant, then focus on the pencil. Repeat several times.

- Move the pencil up, down, from side to side and make slow circles with it. Follow these movements with your eyes. Repeat several times.

- Without the pencil, repeat the above movements several times very slowly.

- Finally, rub your palms together briskly, then cup them over your eyes.

Cold tea bags, cucumber slices or diluted lavender oil on a damp cloth are all very soothing when laid on closed eyelids. You can also bathe your eyes with a cooled herbal infusion of eye-bright and camomile (as advised for PC users).

Eat well
A tight schedule might tempt you to skip meals, eat junk food, or eat absent-mindedly while still writing. These are false economies which you will pay for in brain and body fatigue – and probably digestive disorders – later. Keeping going with stimulants such as alcohol, coffee and tobacco will also have a punishing and detrimental effect on your system.

You owe yourself proper meal breaks – relaxing times spent *away from your desk*, rewarding mind and body for the hard work they have done. How would you feel about a boss who insisted you work through your lunch hour? Don't do it to yourself!

Exercise your joints, muscles, heart and lungs
How would you feel if ordered to sit in one spot for several hours moving only your fingers? Writers regularly submit their bodies to such torture. The long-term results will be stiff joints, atrophied muscles and a variety of other ills which could adversely affect your life – not to mention your creative output.

To redress the balance, add a choice of physical work-outs to your break-time activities list. Work with a yoga, tai chi or keep fit video for example, to ensure that your whole body is exercised and flexibility and strength are maintained.

You also need an aerobic activity, to exercise heart and lungs and send blood and oxygen to all vital organs, including the brain.

Jog, cycle, walk your dogs, dance to Gabrielle Roth, work out with Jane Fonda – whatever you enjoy the most.

Checklist
Your physical health, and therefore your writing, will benefit from:

- good eye care
- eating well
- sleeping well
- breathing deeply
- taking regular breaks
- exercising.

Use physical activity to stimulate your creativity
As mentioned earlier, physical activity often releases a flow of words and ideas. This is probably connected in some way with early development – we learn to use the rest of our bodies before we speak. I saw a striking example of this effect while working on a language-skills programme for children with special needs. The group included an extremely withdrawn eight-year-old boy who had been silent throughout his three years at school.

Having marched round the hall to music, the children wanted to 'march' lying down. As they did so, the boy in question began moving his arms and legs faster and faster against the floor. Suddenly out came a torrent of speech, which increased in speed and volume until he was shouting. Somehow that particular sequence of movements had triggered his speech processes.

Using physical triggers to stimulate the thought processes
Practitioners of therapies like Gestalt and Bioenergetics utilise such physical triggers as enabling mechanisms. Writers can do the same. Crawling, kicking, jumping, punching cushions, even 'marching lying down' can all help words to come. Close the curtains and try it – what have you got to lose?

Writers use a variety of physical triggers to get the creative juices flowing. Veteran sci-fi author Ray Bradbury swims. Charles Schulz, creator of Peanuts, walks or skates. Poet and author Diana Gittins leaps into a boat and rows. Comedy writer Peter Vincent 'gets up from his desk every hour or so to do yoga'. ('Or eat a biscuit,' he adds after some reflection.)

Like many writers, Peter finds that when ideas start flowing he strides about consuming large quantities of food. He also experiences a strong link between his creative process and his physical well-being. He can suffer indigestion and abdominal pain for no apparent reason, make an alteration to the script he is working on and immediately feel fine again – literally a gut reaction.

Checklist

- How does writing affect your body/behaviour?

- What physical activities help you to think better?

Value your health and treat your body well. It is the vehicle of your talent.

Flex your writing muscles

'Get in action,' Natalie Goldberg advises. 'Work it out actively. Pen on paper. Otherwise all your thoughts are dreams. They go nowhere. Let the story move through your hand rather than your head.'

If writing is your main occupation, you probably write daily from necessity. If not it is good to keep the 'writing muscles' flexed in this way. With any discipline, leaving it for a day can lead to several days and so on – until suddenly weeks have passed and you are horribly out of practice. Writing is no different in this respect. You must maintain the momentum if progress is to be made.

Find the time

When we work from the creative rather than the logical mind, the process cannot be rushed. To derive the maximum benefit from the exercises in this book, you need to allow enough time for the experiences to unfold. However, if you find yourself juggling a heap of responsibilities and wondering how you can possibly clear a space for writing, a short regular slot each day is a good compromise solution. Even if you can only manage ten minutes, at the end of the week you will have 70 minutes-worth of writing under your belt. While not ideal, it keeps you writing. In fact a novel per year can be produced in this way.

Go for it
One of the problems with only having ten minutes is that it can take that long just to start thinking. The answer – don't think. Set yourself a time of ten minutes, 20 minutes, an hour – whatever you have available, and just write. 'Get in action.' Keep your hand moving. Whatever comes – no thinking, crossing out, rewriting – just *do* it.

Stick to the allotted time – no more, no less. A timer with an audible signal focuses the mind wonderfully. Some of what you write may be rubbish – fine! When you give yourself permission not to be perfect, things start to happen. At the end of the week look back and highlight the things you might be able to use.

Get started
Write: 'I remember when . . .' or 'I don't remember when . . .' 'I want to tell you about . . .' 'I don't want to tell you about . . .'

Write about a colour, a smell, an emotion. Write about a favourite outfit, an embarrassing experience, a holiday disaster, a beloved pet, a dream. Write about what it feels like to have no ideas.

Write: 'If I were a piece of music I would be . . .' or 'The woman on the bus made me think of . . .'

Open a book or turn on the radio and start with the first sentence you see/hear.

If you get stuck, write your first sentence again and carry on.

Find new ways
Whether you are doing timed writing, taking notes or first-drafting, writing in a linear way from left to right is only one of many choices. Try writing round the edges, starting in the middle, writing in columns, spirals, flower-shapes – whatever takes your fancy.

I find linear note-taking of little use for recovering information afterwards. I prefer to 'chunk' my thoughts (see Figure 1) so that they leap off the page, demanding my attention. I draw a shape around each chunk as I write, to keep them separate. (The doodles come later when I am thinking.)

I also like to organise my writer's notebook in this way. When I dot snatches of conversation, description and thoughts around the page, I find they come together in ways I might not have thought of if I had used linear jotting.

I also find coloured paper and pens useful – and fun. They

alleviate boredom, evoke a particular mood, and help me organise my thoughts.

Checklist

- Set a time and keep to it.

- Decide how you want to position the words on the page.

- Choose a starting sentence and return to it if stuck.

- Don't stop until the time is up.

- Don't think, cross out, rewrite – just do it.

Timed writing as a daily practice

Many writers, whatever their situation, find daily timed writing useful. If you are short of time, it can help bypass any panic engendered by a blank sheet of paper and a ticking clock.

When time is not a problem, it can help combat that perverse ailment, 'don't want to start'. Having moved mountains to clear a day – or a life – in which to write, many of us are suddenly afflicted with a paralysing torpor. This can be because self-motivation is new to us (see 'Organising your work time' below) or because of self-doubt (see 'Writing and your identity' below). Timed writing cuts through both by a) giving you something definite to do and b) setting no standards.

Try: 'I am now going to write as badly as I can for ten minutes'.

Timed writing also clears mental 'dross' so that the good stuff can start to flow – like priming a pump. It is the equivalent of a performer's or athlete's warm-up exercises. It can also produce something amazing in its own right.

Keep a notebook by your bed and do your timed writing before even getting up. This is an excellent way to kick-start your writing day.

Checklist

Timed writing can help you:

- focus

- clear your mind

- warm up

- get started.

WRITING AND YOUR LIFESTYLE

'To nurture your talent requires considerable discipline, for there are many other good things you will not have time to do if you are serious about your creativity.'

(Marilee Zedenek: *The Right Brain Experience*)

There are also many not-so-good things which you will not have time to do – or may feel forced to do instead.

How important is writing to you?

List all your current projects and activities. Rate the significance of each one on a scale of 1–10, then list them again in order of importance.

- Where does writing come on this list?

- How does this affect the way you feel about your workspace and work time?

Organise your workspace

Do you need silence or do you, like Peter Ustinov, find it unbearable? Do you need to be free from distractions, or can you work at the kitchen table while your two-year-old plays football with the saucepans? Do you need everything neatly labelled and filed, or do you prefer cheerful clutter? How important is the decor?

- Take a few moments to imagine your ideal workspace – no restrictions.

- Make this workspace the subject of a five-minute timed writing.

- In your present circumstances, how close can you come to that ideal?

- Make this compromise workspace the subject of a second timed writing.

Claim your territory

You may have to share this space with others. How protective do you feel about the area or areas you use?

Fig. 1.   'Chunked' notes from a story-telling workshop.

- How do you mark your boundaries so that others do not encroach on them?

- Are you clear about your needs for space and privacy?

- How assertive are you in defending these needs?

For many of us this territorial aspect of the workspace is very important, and needs addressing. Having to worry that papers might be moved, read, damaged – even accidentally thrown away – is a most unwelcome distraction.

If you have your own work room, are you making full use of the freedom this allows you? Has it dawned on you that you can do *anything you like* in there? For example, writing on the walls and ceiling can be very liberating – perhaps chunking ideas (as in Figure 1). The result feels amazing – like sitting inside your brain.

Take a few moments to think about ways of using your space more creatively.

Go walkabout
Having organised your workspace and settled in, make sure it does not eventually become a new rut. Try working somewhere else occasionally – a change of scene can help ideas to flow. Even a different part of the house can feel surprisingly adventurous when you have got used to one particular location.

If you really want to trigger your imagination, try some of the places you chose in childhood – behind the sofa, in a wardrobe, in the cupboard under the stairs. (Does this sound like a daft idea? Would it help to know that at least two well-known and respected authors write underneath their dining room tables?)

> 'People try to become everything except a song. They want to become rich, powerful, famous. But – they lose all qualities that can make their life joyous; they lose all cheerfulness, they become serious.'
>
> (Osho: *Morning Contemplation*)

Wanting to be somewhere else
Do you sometimes feel you need to be somewhere else entirely – but if you manage to get there, find it is not right either? Does isolation make you long for company and vice versa? Do you rent a cottage by the sea, and end up writing in a café in the centre of town? 'I thought it was only me!' other writers will probably say if

you ever confess. It is possible that this yearning for something we cannot have is a necessary part of the creative process.

Once, when writing a certain story, I felt compelled to stay in a seaside boarding house up north, in winter. The arrangements I had to make in order to do so were considerable. I stuck it for one day. Now I use my imagination to go where I yearn to go. This is quicker, cheaper and far less disappointing.

Organise your work time

Does your time feel as though it is structured for you, or do you set your own schedule? We have seen how timed writing can help in both situations. We have also looked at scheduling a writing day around regular breaks.

If you are used to working for someone else, both motivation and time-management may feel difficult at first. The leisure-time writing habit may also be difficult to kick, so that you find you are writing all day, every day and exhausting yourself. Is this something you need to change?

Whether you are fitting writing in or fitting other things in around writing, some organisational skill will be needed. As with your workspace, your work time will need to be claimed and marked out in some way. The people around you will need to know any 'rules' that apply to the time when you are writing.

If you live alone, make your writing hours known to friends, neighbours or anyone else who might call round. Place a 'do not disturb' notice on the front door if necessary.

- Think about any areas of tension affecting your writing time. How can you reduce these?

- Do a five-minute timed writing about the steps you will take to achieve this.

Research

Does your schedule allow plenty of time for any research you need to do? How do you feel about research? It need not mean hours spent in the library. Active research, immersing yourself in the place where your story is to be set, is likely to be more enjoyable and will help you to bring the setting to life for your readers.

Novelist Marjorie Darke recommends conversing with 'anyone in the locality who can increase my background knowledge'. She also aims to share as many of her characters' experiences as possible. While researching *Ride the Iron Horse*, for example, she took part in a traction engine race. Similarly, Peter Vincent spent many hours as a leisure centre user while doing initial research for *The Brittas Empire*, and Canadian writer Jo Davis thoroughly indulged her passion for trains while working on *Not a Sentimental Journey*.

Novelist Alison Harding describes research as 'a sort of radar that picks up on things you need to know and draws your attention to them'. This radar also seems to work subliminally. Alison, in common with a number of writers, has often had the experience of inventing a happening in relation to a certain place, researching the location and finding that a similar event actually occurred there.

Reading

Make sure your schedule also includes plenty of time for reading – particularly the type of material you like to write. In order to be part of the 'writing world', you need to know what is happening in your chosen field. What appeals to you? What is selling? Who is publishing it?

A particular joy of being a writer is that you can feel positively virtuous about being an obsessive reader.

Checklist

• What do you need in terms of time and space for writing?

• How can you best make sure these needs are met?

• How will you make this clear to those around you?

• What role might your imagination play?

• Have you allowed plenty of time for reading and other research?

Stay in touch with the rest of the world

One of writing's many paradoxes is that it is an isolated activity through which we reach out to others. It is a way of making our voice heard in the world.

So how might the other half of that dialogue be conducted – by reading the papers, watching the news, talking? Do you read your first drafts to others and value their response – or do you prefer to internalise the energy at this stage? Whatever your choice, the most important question is *does it work for you*?

YOUR WRITER'S TOOL KIT

Essential items

Look at – or imagine – your workspace. List the things you simply could not do without. Is yours a Zen-like existence – just a pad and pencil, or is your room overflowing? Would you like to add or discard things, or is it fine the way it is?

How do you feel about the suggestion that our surroundings reflect our inner state? Some people with crowded workspaces worry that their brain might be 'cluttered'. Do you? Perhaps your brain is more like a handbag than an orderly bookshelf. Think of it as overflowing with useful things which you can grab whenever you want them.

If you are not happy with the contents of your workspace (or your handbag) list those things again in order of priority and see whether you can discard some. Or do you need to acquire more? If the latter, read on. Otherwise skip the next two sections – you might be tempted.

Highly useful items

- Thesaurus. Dictionaries of proverbs and quotations. Rhyming dictionary.

- Current encyclopaedia for checking dates and information.

- Books of names.

- Hand-held cassette recorder for dictating as an alternative means of recording your words. (Try timed dictation as an alternative to timed writing.)

- For PC users, a voice-operated word processor as an alternative to the above.

- A large clock and a timer with an audible signal.

- Kettle, cup, tea etc – leaving the room to make drinks can be distracting.

- Answering machine and/or fax.

Treats
These are important. Here are a few suggestions.

Aromatherapy oils in a burner or applied (suitably diluted) to the skin. Try: pine for inspiration, sage for opening to the subconscious, lavender, camomile and rose to relax, grapefruit to wake up, geranium to stimulate dreams.

For a wonderful 'quick-fix', place a drop of oil on the centre of each palm, rub them together vigorously, then cup your hands over your nose and inhale deeply (many thanks to aromatherapist Ruth Wise for that idea).

You might prefer to reward yourself with a large bar of **chocolate**, kept by a partner or friend and delivered at a specific time – with a cup of tea perhaps. Or a long **soak in the bath** might be more your style.

How about a large **comfy chair** to snuggle into for hand-drafting or reading?

Items for writing 'the right brain way'
The uses for these will be explained in subsequent chapters:

- tarot cards in your preferred style and tradition

- coloured pens and papers

- mirror

- magnifying glass, binoculars

- tape recorder

- small dictionary

- basic astrology text or programme (optional).

WRITING AND YOUR IDENTITY

Invent yourself as a writer
Your writing self may well express an aspect of your personality which is normally hidden from the world. Perhaps you have a high-powered job which requires you to be very 'left-brain', while your writing self is poetic and vulnerable. Or the reverse – you write horror, crime or erotic fiction and teach infants by day. Perhaps you write as a person of the opposite gender.

In order to manage any tension between these different facets of yourself, or to prevent one popping out at an inappropriate time, try 'fleshing them out', much as you would one of your characters. Perhaps one of the functions of a pen-name is to allow the writing self and the everyday self to lead separate lives.

Value yourself and your writing

How do you feel about writing as an occupation? When you talk about it, do you feel proud – or embarrassed? Do you use the words 'only' or 'just' when you describe your work? Do you call it 'scribbling'? Do you think of writing as a 'proper' job? Do you feel justified in claiming time and space to do it? How do you feel about the writing you produce? Are you confident enough to submit it to publishers? How do you cope with rejection slips?

Have feelings about yourself as a writer affected your attitude to any of the suggestions in this chapter? For example, do you feel it is worth following the physical programme, setting up a work-space, claiming time, collecting a 'tool kit'? Are other things/other people 'more important'? Do you feel you are kidding yourself that you can do this?

It may be a while before you can give positive answers to these questions and really mean it – but with perseverance it happens. An 'invented self' can be a huge help in this respect. A self that is feeling positive and strong can give the less confident one a pep-talk.

A supportive attitude from those close to you is also invaluable. A friend at the beginning of her writing career heard her husband tell a caller, 'My wife is a writer and cannot be disturbed'. She felt she could do anything after that.

CASE STUDIES

Karen only has a few minutes

Karen has two young children and works part-time as a computer programmer. As a teenager, she wrote short stories and poetry. For years she has been trying to find time to do this again, but somehow it never happens. She has now decided that ten minutes a day would be considerably better than nothing. She will spend ten minutes of her lunch break writing – in her car to make sure she is not disturbed. She used to write in the garden shed when she was a child, and rather fancies trying it again if she gets a chance.

David has plenty of time on his hands

David has recently been made redundant from his job as office manager. He has always wanted to write a crime novel, and plans to make use of his time at home to do so. He has organised his writing day with as much care and precision as he used in running his office. He realises the importance of reading novels in his chosen genre, and has set aside a regular time slot for this. He has also allowed plenty of time for research. He is not too sure about things like aromatherapy and writing in cupboards, but he can see the value of a good health programme. He has tried timed writing and found it useful.

Sheila finds it hard to get organised – is she avoiding something?

Sheila's children have left home, but there still seem to be many demands on her time. She is a school governor, serves on three committees, sings in a choir, and does volunteer work in a hospital.

  She has had stories published in women's magazines, and once had a play accepted for radio although it was never performed. She would like to write more, but finds her days too broken up with various activities to really marshal her thoughts. Recently she has begun to wonder whether she is avoiding writing in case she cannot do it well enough.

2

Tune in

As writers we need to fine-tune our senses to both our inner and outer worlds. Whether we are observing people, objects, locations or situations an important part of the process is paying close attention to what is happening *within ourselves* as we do so. Our inner experience of the world is what we communicate to others in our writing, so it is important to be aware of ourselves and our feelings.

TUNE IN TO YOURSELF

The following exercises will help you to develop this vital skill.

Focus inwards

Become still. Let your breathing settle. Take your awareness inwards.

- What is your life like at this moment? Allow an image to emerge. Do not try to hurry it up. Take time to let the image develop and reveal itself.

- What particular aspect of your life do you think this image represents? How do you feel about it?

- When you have finished exploring this image, draw it. Get to know it even better. Would you like to change it in any way?

Tune in physically

First, read the instructions for this exercise onto a tape. Remember to pause for at least one minute after each instruction, to allow the experience to unfold. Play back the tape and do the exercise with eyes closed.

- Allow one hand to explore the other – slowly, carefully, as though it were an unfamiliar object. Notice the temperature, the texture, the different shapes.

- Which hand is doing the exploring? How does it feel in that exploring role?

- Transfer your attention now to the hand that is being explored. How does that feel? Focus on those feelings about being explored.

- Change the roles over. How does each hand feel now?

- If your right hand had a voice, what would it sound like? What would it say?

- Give your left hand a voice. What sort of voice is it? What does it say?

- Let your hands talk to each other for a while.

- Open your eyes. Record your experiences.

Did it feel strange to focus on yourself in that way? This is a very useful habit for writers to develop. Feelings about ourselves often influence our treatment of characters. See what links you notice in this respect after completing the next exercise.

Tune in to your self-image
Do this quickly, with as little thought as possible.

- Write the numbers 1–10 underneath each other 'shopping list' style.

- Beside each number write **one** word which describes you.

- Put this list aside. Do something else for ten minutes.

- Now, on a fresh sheet of paper, write the numbers 1–10 again.

- With your **other hand** write ten words which describe you.

- Compare the two lists.

Did you find some of your words positive and some negative? Did you contradict yourself, even in the same list? Did the lists reflect different, perhaps contradictory, aspects of your personality?

Tune in to an internal dialogue

- Writing with each hand in turn, set up a dialogue about yourself.

- Ask questions about any aspects of your life that have been puzzling or annoying you. Let one hand ask and the other one answer.

Discover the critic within

Writing with the non-dominant hand, as we did in the last two exercises, puts us in the 'child place'. It can bring up feelings of vulnerability and frustration, making us impatient with ourselves. We may find ourselves thinking that exercises like these are just gimmicks or tricks which cannot produce anything 'truly creative'. Such reactions are often due to unhelpful messages we received about ourselves in childhood – messages which have stuck and which cause us to criticise ourselves today.

Once we recognise these 'old tapes' for what they are, we can learn to turn them off. 'Not today, thank you,' 'What's *your* problem?' or simply 'Shut up!' are some of the more polite ways of dealing with these internal voices. Tracing such messages to a specific individual, going back in your imagination and delivering the message personally can be a very liberating experience.

Bypass the critic

The physical difficulty of writing with the non-dominant hand, distracts us from the words themselves. It is therefore an excellent way to bypass our internal critic. We are then free to rediscover the spontaneous creativity of childhood, and surprise ourselves with the results.

Word association activities also enable us to bypass the critic, provided we allow ourselves to let go and write whatever comes into our heads. The two word-association exercises which follow are useful tools at any stage in the writing process. In this case they will be used for tuning in to ourselves.

Word web

- In the centre of a clean sheet of A3 or A4 paper, write one word from the lists you made in the second exercise. Circle it.

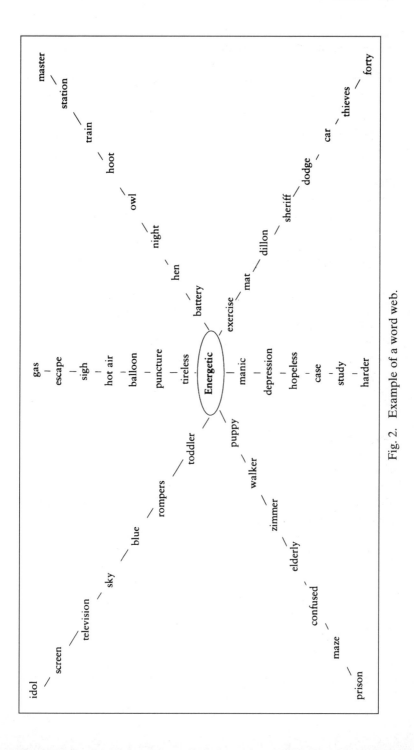

Fig. 2. Example of a word web.

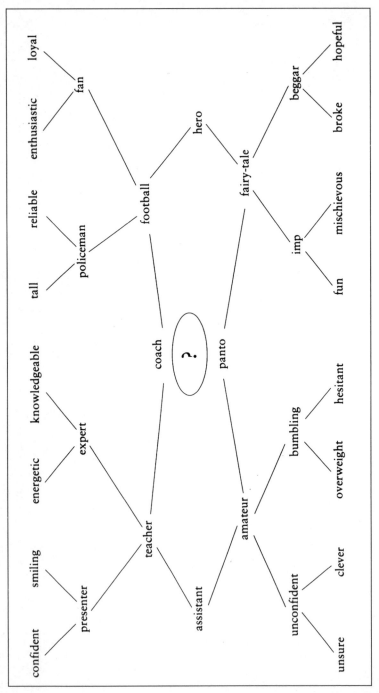

Fig. 3. A word honeycomb.

- Radiating from this circle, draw six short 'spokes' (see Figure 2) and at the end of each spoke write a word you associate with the word in the centre.

- From each of these six words, quickly write a succession of associated words, continuing each spoke to the edge of the page.

- Now let your eye roam around the page. Soon words will begin to group themselves into unexpected phrases. For example, the 'energetic' person in Figure 2 might come to life on the page as a *manic walker* with an *exercise mat* in their *back-pack*, a *forty*-year-old *battery hen* or even a *balloon* in *blue rompers*. Such phrases are unlikely to result from logical thinking processes.

Word webs move outwards from a central idea. The next technique moves inwards from a number of ideas towards a central focus.

Word honeycomb

- In the centre of an A3 or A4 sheet, circle a space for a word. Leave it empty.

- Choose 16 words from the lists you made in the second exercise. Write eight along the top edge and the others along the bottom (see Figure 3).

- Starting with the top line, find a word which connects the first two words and write it below with two connecting lines, as shown. Find a word to connect words 3 and 4, 5 and 6, 7 and 8.

- From the new line formed, find a word to connect words 1 and 2, 3 and 4, positioning them below, as before.

- Find a connecting word for the two words in the new line, and write it above the space you have marked out.

- Repeat this process, working upwards from the bottom of the page.

- Taking the third line from the top and the third line from the bottom, find a word to connect the two words on the left (*teacher* and *amateur* in Figure 3) and another to connect the two words on the right (*football* and *fairytale*). Write them on either side of the marked space, as shown.

- Find a word or a person which connects all four central words, as shown.

In Figure 3, the words *coach* and *panto* suggest 'Cinderella'. This could lead us to *Buttons* as the *assistant hero* in that story. Someone with this result might ask themselves, 'How am I like Buttons? Am I a good friend? Do I sometimes keep a low profile – and am I happy with that? How am I not like Buttons at all?'

Like the characters in our dreams, the characters we invent in our writing reflect aspects of ourselves – whether we are aware of it or not. Active engagement with this process enables us to know our characters intimately and therefore transfer them convincingly to the page.

Checklist

- What have you learned about yourself through doing these exercises?

- How will you use this in your writing?

- What have you learned about your internal critic?

- How will you deal with your critic in future?

- How will you use word association and writing with the non-dominant hand?

TUNE IN TO YOUR CHARACTERS

Use what you know

As suggested above, the first step to knowing your characters is knowing yourself. Ask 'how am I like/unlike this person? How do I feel about them? Who do they remind me of?' Write some of the answers with your non-dominant hand.

Next, choose one word to describe this character. Make it the centre of a web. Or use both hands to make two eight-word lists, then build a honeycomb.

CLOTHES	Homemade	Too pretty	Old fashioned	Wants jeans	Hides DMs at Gran's	Hates bonnets	Holes in socks	Nurse's outfit	Two of everything	Matching knickers
MOODS	'Sweet'	Catty	Unpredictable	Fed up	Vulnerable	Stormy	Rebellious	Co-operative	Trusting	Devious
FOOD	Loves chocolate	Allergic to nuts	Hates tomatoes	Like bread	Loves jam sandwiches	Apples are OK	Goes hyper on oranges	Swallows prune pits	Feeds cat spinach	Bakes own cakes
COLOURS	Favourite is blue	Hates red	Wants to wear black	Paints in pastels	Dyes hair purple	Likes stripes	Hates checks	Hates brown	Painted room pink	Has pink duvet
FRIENDS	Lucille Locket	Bridie O'Peep	M. Muffett (Spinster)	Call her 'Rosie'	Live some way away	Take advantage	Don't often visit	Gossip about her	She wants new ones	Has put ad in paper
PETS	Budgie	Goldfish	Snake	Tarantula	Keeps in bedroom	Allergic to fur	Would like a duck	Animals like her	Wants a pig	Hates poodles
MUSIC	Plays the piano	Can't sing	Wants a drum set	Likes Oasis	Mother likes Cliff	Hates opera	Likes heavy metal	Loves string quartets	Writes her songs	Dad plays Concertina
HOBBIES	Reading Sci-Fi	Painting	Embroidery	Knitting	Listening to Radio 2	Planning robberies	Dying hair	Trying out make-up	Plays drums in a band	Wind-surfing
TALENTS	Good with animals	Good listener	Tastes good	Good cook	Good seamstress	Good with colours	Musical ability	Persuasive talker	Leadership potential	Criminal potential
FLAWS	Thinks she can sing	Over-confident	Gullible	Short-sighted	Vain	Quick temper	Abrasive	Untruthful	Eats too much	Secret drinker

Fig. 4. A 10 × 10: Red Riding Hood.

Use your imagination . . .

. . . to converse with your character
Tune in to this person's speech. How do they sound? What gestures do they use? What is their accent like?

- Imagine they are sitting opposite you, and talk to them.

- Write a dialogue between this character and a character who represents some aspect of yourself – your left-hand self maybe, or your internal critic. Is the speech of each character quite distinct, or is it sometimes unclear which one of you is speaking? How can you improve on this?

. . . to do five-minute writings about your character
'If this person were . . . an animal, a flower, a fruit, a piece of music – what would it be?'
'I don't know anything about their . . . but I imagine . . .'
'If they found themselves . . . on a desert island/naked at a concert/ having tea with the Queen, they would . . .'
'When this person makes a cup of tea/mows the lawn, they . . .'
(Choose any everyday task, not necessarily appropriate to the character's period. Heathcliff doing the weekly shop, for example, could be quite revealing.)

. . . to do a 10 x 10
Make a grid, ten spaces down and ten across, big enough to write a few words in each space. Down the side of the grid list ten aspects of a character's life: clothes, musical tastes, favourite food, pet hates etc.

With the minimum of thought, fill in the grid by brainstorming ten facts about each of those aspects (see Figure 4). You now have 100 facts about your character.

Because you did not consider them carefully first, some of these things may seem quite off-the-wall. Good. These are probably the ones which will make the character live – the unexpected or secret things which make him or her unique.

You will not use all these facts when you write about the character – but you will *know* them. This will make the character feel more and more alive to you.

Discover more

Left side/right side
Most people's faces reveal different personality traits on each side. These often represent the self they show the world and the more hidden self.

Ask a friend or partner to cover each half of their face in turn. Describe what you see each time. Compare the two descriptions. Were you surprised?

Repeat the exercise with any full-face photograph. Now place a mirror down the centre of the face to view the wholly left-sided/right-sided person.

Repeat the exercise with a full-face photograph of somebody who resembles your character. This is another way to make your characters multi-dimensional.

Guided visualisation
Tape these instructions and listen to them in a relaxed state with closed eyes. Speak slowly, leaving sufficient pauses for the experience to unfold. Switch the tape off and make notes at intervals to suit yourself.

Bring your character into your awareness. Visualise them in every detail. Notice their size, their shape, the way they stand or sit . . . About how old are they? When you have a clear picture in your mind, try to hear the character's voice . . .

What sort of mood are they in? What is the first thing they might say to you? Try being your character for a while. Take on their mood . . .

Look down at the clothes you are wearing . . . How do they feel against your skin? Who chose these clothes? Are you happy in them?

Stand like the character . . . walk like them . . . sit like them.

What does this person smell like? Is it the smell of their house or workplace?

What is this person's house like? Is it clean and tidy, or in a muddle? Do they have any pets? What do the different parts of the house smell like? What can you hear as you move around this house?

What can you see out of the windows? Are there any neighbours? How does this person get on with the people living nearby? Who visits the house? Who does this person visit?

What did they have for breakfast today? How did they eat it? What is this person's attitude to food in general?

How do they spend their time? How do they enjoy themselves – and when?

Add any other questions you need to ask.

You may already have a name for your character. If not, tune in again and ask them. Also ask how they feel about that name and who chose it.

How do you feel about the character now?

Use tarot cards

Tarot cards represent powerful archetypal energies – the collective human experience underlying legend, myth and folklore. Many types and styles of deck are available from book stores and 'New Age' shops, and through mail or Internet order. Used with respect, the tarot offers insight into our own lives and those of our characters.

Separate from the rest of the pack the cards depicting people. From these, either select one which reminds you of your character, or place the cards face downwards before choosing, thus inviting fate to take a hand.

If you chose the card consciously, note your reasons for doing so. Then write down everything both observed and imagined about the character on the card. Use some of the techniques you have learned in this chapter to help you.

Note any surprises. Look at the card for a while. Let it 'speak' to you.

If you chose the card at random, consider it as an aspect of the character of which you were unaware. Work with it as above. Alternatively, choose from the whole pack, with the chance of considering your character as an animal, object or place – as in the timed writing above. Or choose a card to represent a new character entirely.

Many tarot sets come with a manual, and this will provide additional insight.

Use unexpected juxtaposition

Word webs jolt us out of our language rut by placing words in unusual groupings. Placing our characters in unaccustomed social or geographical settings has a similar effect (see '. . . to do five-minute writings about your character', page 36).

How would:

- Captain Kirk control a class of infants?

- Spock organise the teas at a church garden fête?

- David Copperfield relate to Jane Eyre, or Robinson Crusoe to Ophelia?

Write one of your characters into a scene from your favourite novel. What can you learn about them from their reactions? (For parents and teachers of teenagers: revitalise flagging interest in a set book by the introduction of a favourite TV character, eg Scully from the X-files visits Pride and Prejudice.)

Draw a tarot card at random and get your character to interact with the person, place or situation depicted. Pay particular attention to the dialogue.

Checklist

Bring your characters to life by:

- asking how they are like/unlike you, and exploring your feelings about them

- talking with them

- using word webs, honeycombs, timed writing and '10 × 10'

- considering both sides of their face/character

- using guided visualisation

- using tarot cards

- putting the character in an unaccustomed setting.

TUNE IN TO AN OBJECT

Focusing on an object usually indicates either its significance to the plot, or its relationship to one of the characters. The condition of an object may provide clues to a person's lifestyle or may be used as a metaphor for their mood.

Techniques for tuning into ourselves and into a character can also be used for tuning into an object. Also, ask who found it or made it, when and where. Invent a history for its finder/maker and imagine its journey from the point of origin to the point at which it arrived in our story.

Another very useful technique is to speak as the object, in the first person: 'I am a grubby white telephone – much used, pawed, put down, buttons pressed, never really seen by anyone . . .' and so on.

This will tell you things about your character or yourself, and may also start you off on a completely new story.

TUNE IN TO SETTINGS

Again, most of the techniques described so far can be used in relation to a setting. Speaking as the setting in the first person is particularly effective when landscape and weather are seen as reflective of a character's mood.

Use alternate hands to dialogue with the landscape. When you have a name for the place, use this as the centre of a web.

Tarot cards are also very useful, whether you work directly with a setting or choose another type of card to use as a metaphor.

Timed writing
Think of a setting you have experienced which is similar to the one in your story. Begin 'I remember . . .' and write for ten minutes. 'I don't remember . . .' also brings up some interesting details.

Guided visualisation
Tape, as before. Listen in a relaxed state with closed eyes.

Find yourself in the location of your story. Really feel you are there . . .
What time of day is it? Are there people around? Animals? What is the weather like? What time of year is it? What historical period?
Start to explore . . . look . . . touch . . . Feel the air against

your skin. What can you hear? . . . smell? Can you taste anything?

What is the atmosphere of this place? Do you feel comfortable here?

What is the pace like – lively? Slow? Is it in tune with your mood?

What is the name of this place? See it written on a sign saying 'Welcome to . . .'

Take another walk around. Find a door or a road or pathway that you have not noticed before. Where does it leads you?

TUNE IN TO A SITUATION

The Mythic and the Osho Zen tarot decks vividly depict a variety of situations. Work with them as you did with characters and settings. Describe what you see, record your feelings (writing with both hands if appropriate), let the card 'speak'. Use webs, honeycombs, and timed writing. Consult the manuals for further insight. Many newspaper photographs also capture the essence of the moment and are a very good resource for tuning in, using the techniques described.

Create tension and mystery

Work outdoors
Use binoculars. Imagine you are watching a film. Survey the territory, then suddenly focus on one feature. Imagine the soundtrack playing a couple of loud chords. The feature immediately assumes huge significance and your imagination turns a somersault.

Work with a picture
Use a magnifying glass and a printed picture with a reasonable amount of detail (eg a photograph, postcard, or picture from a magazine or holiday brochure). Let your eye roam over the picture, then suddenly magnify a car – an open window – a clock on a steeple – a group of people. Each time, imagine an appropriately attention-grabbing soundtrack. What could it mean?

Make one of these magnified features the subject of a five-minute timed writing.

Checklist
New techniques:

- speak as an object or setting, in the first person
- use a magnifying glass or binoculars.

CASE STUDIES

Karen finds it difficult to concentrate
Karen finds that she can use her snatched moments in the car for timed writing, but not for tuning in and guided visualisation. Eventually she clears a regular slot when the children are in bed, unplugs the phone and puts a 'do not disturb' notice on the front door. She lets friends and family know that she will not be available during that time. She also writes in the garden shed when the children are playing at a friend's house. She is amazed at how it helps her poetry.

David feels silly at first
David finds this way of working strange, and feels foolish about exploring his feelings and writing about himself with his left hand. He gets angry and wants to give up. Discovering his internal critic helps him to understand where these feelings come from. After getting some good results from word webs and successfully using a honeycomb to find out whodunit, he decides to persevere.

Sheila wishes she had found this way of working earlier
When Sheila finally organises some clear days for writing, she is surprised at how enjoyable it is, and at how it flows. As she suspected, she had been putting it off in case she was unable to do it well enough. She thinks the fact that the BBC decided not to perform her play may have affected her more than she realised. The techniques help her to rediscover playfulness. She is excited by the way her stories start to unfold, and wishes she had tried it earlier.

3

Discover the Plot

Sometimes we begin with a very clear idea of the plot but only a hazy idea about the characters and setting. We then have to spend time 'tuning in' in various ways in order to get to know them. Sometimes the reverse happens – a character or a place really grabs our attention, and we wonder what their story might be. Sometimes the plot which seemed so clear suddenly takes an unexpected turn 'all by itself'.

Once we are aware of these processes we can make them work for us, so that we can follow a plot as it unfolds, rather than struggle to think what comes next.

WHOSE STORY IS IT ANYWAY?

Use the following guided visualisations to develop a new plot, or to work on a current one. Tape the three sets of instructions first with appropriate pauses (as in Chapter 2).

- If this is new work, choose a character from your tarot pack or writer's notebook and spend some time tuning in to them.

- If you wish to work on a current project, let one of the main characters come into your mind. Take some time to reacquaint yourself fully with this character before proceeding to the exercise.

- Have your writing materials near to hand, *or*

- Respond aloud to the questions. Record the whole journey, including your responses, on a second tape recorder.

Guided visualisation 1
Bring your character fully into your awareness now.
What does their face and their posture tell you about their

mood? Ask them what has happened to them today. Where have they been? Who have they met?

Was it an unusual, or an average day? How has it left them feeling?

Become this person now. Step into their skin, their clothing. Begin to move as they move, and speak as they speak.

What can you see around you? What can you hear, feel, smell, taste?

Notice the qualities of the light, the temperature and humidity. How does it feel to be in that place?

Find somewhere to sit quietly and reflect on your day and the events which led up to it. Gradually let your mind move backwards over your life, so that the events leading up to what happened here, today, in this place, become clear to you. Notice your feelings as you do this.

How do you see today in terms of your life as a whole? What do you think might happen next? How are you feeling now?

When you are ready, open your eyes.

- Write as your character in the first person. Make these experiences the subject of a ten-minute timed writing. Begin 'The story of my life has been . . .'

Guided visualisation 2

When you are ready, close your eyes and return to the place where you met your character.

Your character is not here. Spend some time exploring on your own.

Someone is approaching. You can see them nearby. They want to make contact.

This person likes to gossip. They are eager to tell you their version of the events which your character described earlier. Listen to what they have to say. Ask any questions you want to ask, but do not argue.

When you are ready, draw this conversation to a close, take your leave of the gossiping person and open your eyes.

- As the gossip, in the first person, write your version of the events you have just described. Record your feelings as you write. When you are ready, close your eyes and return to that place.

Guided visualisation 3
Almost immediately a person approaches. They are anxious to talk with you. It becomes clear that this is a person in whom your character has confided. They can be trusted. They have news of what is happening to your character now. Listen carefully. Ask whether your character needs your help in any way.
The trusted friend also wants to put the record straight about what the gossip told you. Discuss this with them for a while. Make sure you now have the correct information. When you are ready, draw this conversation to a close, thank the trusted friend, take your leave of them and open your eyes.

- So what really happened? Write a dialogue between the gossip and the trusted friend. Use two different coloured pens. Try writing with both hands.

Outline the plot
Write a brief resume of the story so far. What overall theme is developing? Choose *one* or, at the most, *two* words to describe the key theme(s) of your story. Imagine a snappy description on a book jacket: 'This is a story of . . . and . . .'

Here are some suggestions:

adventure	betrayal	brutality	courage
disintegration	discovery	disempowerment	disgust
escape	envy	fanaticism	fear
frustration	greed	growth	hatred
inequality	jealousy	justice	innocence
intimidation	loss	love	mystery
obsession	power	pride	purpose
punishment	pursuit	rebellion	recovery
release	rescue	revenge	sacrifice
search	secrets	selfishness	shame
temptation	transformation	trickery	victory

Precisely identifying the theme in this way keeps your writing focused. This is particularly important when writing a short story. Keep returning to the theme and checking it out: 'This is a story about x and y – am I making this clear? Am I reinforcing this theme, or am I losing the impact by getting side-tracked?'

Checklist

- Let your character tell their story and their feelings about it.
- Let other characters tell you their version.
- Briefly outline the story as you see it.
- Identify the key theme(s).
- Keep returning to the key themes and checking them out.

INVENT AN AUDIENCE

As soon as preparations are complete and the real story telling begins, we need an audience: initially one specific person to whom we can direct our thoughts. Without this externalised third party, our writing can become a private conversation with our characters. Our reader may feel like a late arrival at a party, bewildered and excluded.

Increasing introspection can also cause us to lose sight of our ideas – as if they have disappeared into a black hole. This particular manifestation of so-called 'writer's block' can often be reversed by focusing our thoughts outwards again.

- Take a few minutes to write about a recent event in your life.
- Now write 'Dear . . .' and describe the same event in a letter to a friend.
- What differences did you notice?

Who would you like to be the recipient of your story? Will it be someone you know, or someone you invent? What do you need from them?

If your story is intended for a specific market, say a particular women's magazine, visualise one representative of that audience. Use a guided journey, left-hand writing, webs, 10 × 10 etc to become fully acquainted with this person, then deliver your story just to them.

If your priority at this stage is to tell your story clearly, invent your listener as one of those irritating people who asks a question after every few sentences. If style and quality are your main concern, invent someone who is not easily satisfied, who expects the best from you and wants you to get it just right. Remember – they are there for your benefit. Choose the audience which you will find most stimulating and enabling.

- Try different listeners at different stages in the story's development.

- Invite your listener to contribute to the story.

- Tarot cards, family photographs, china ducks – anything, can be your audience.

- Switch roles and *be* the audience. Have your say from this seat too.

Checklist

Inventing an audience enables you to:

- focus

- direct your ideas outwards

- consider your readers' needs

- tell your story clearly

- gain a new perspective.

PLAYING ALL THE PARTS

Swiss psychoanalyst and mystic, Carl Jung suggests that everything we dream represents an aspect of ourselves. If we dream we are having tea with a cat in a pink swimsuit, we are the cat, the swimsuit, the tea, the place where the tea is served and so on. When we work with a dream, insight can be obtained by communicating with or becoming each of these parts in turn (see Chapter 7 for further information).

Doing this with our visualisations gives us many new viewpoints to work with.

Either tape your responses to the following exercise or make them the subject of timed writing.

- Return to the first visualisation in this chapter. Find yourself again in the setting where you met your character. Notice the things around you. Talk with them.

- Speak as each of the objects in turn now. Speak as the character's clothing and footwear. Tell the story from each of these points of view.

Checklist
Playing all the parts enables us to:

- get the most out of our visualisations

- gain new insight and new perspectives.

LET FATE TAKE A HAND

Games of chance
Introducing an element of chance, injects new life into our characters, our plot – and us.

Scrabble
1. Play a 15-minute game, either by yourself or with a friend. At the end of that time, write a story using every word on the board.
2. Or instead of recording the scores, record each word. Use them in the order in which they appeared.
3. Alternatively, use only the nouns or only the verbs which appeared. Make each one the focus of a stage in your plot. Supposing the verbs you made were:
   plan   pack   doubt   arrange   saw   spend

   A sample plot outline could read:

- Emily **plans** to surprise her husband Tim with a party on their anniversary.
- She tells him to keep that day free. 'I **doubt** I shall be here,' he says.

- He starts to **spend** a lot of time away from home and seems preoccupied.
- A friend tells Emily that she **saw** Tim coming out of a hotel with his secretary.
- Devastated, Emily cancels the party and **packs** her case to leave.
- Tim has been planning to celebrate their anniversary with a second honeymoon. His secretary has been helping him to **arrange** it.

Snakes and Ladders

Throw the dice and move a counter accordingly. Whatever number you land on, take a dictionary or choose a book at random and open it at that page. Close your eyes and point to a word. Use it in your opening sentence. Continue in this way for each sentence. If you go up a ladder, let something positive occur in your character's life. If you go down a snake, introduce an obstacle or misfortune.

The story ends after a set number of throws, or when you reach the last square.

- If you have a Monopoly set, try using the 'Chance' and 'Community Chest' cards when you encounter a ladder or a snake.

- Draw a Tarot card if you land on a snake, a ladder or any number divisible by five.

Any dice and counter board game can be adapted in this way – or you can make your own game board to suit your needs.

Dice

1. Use a pair of dice and a dictionary. Devise your own word finding rules. For example, the first throw gives you a page number, the second tells you where it comes on that page (1st 2nd etc). Or, choose a word at random, throw the dice, count forward that number of words and use the word you land on. Throw again to find the next word and so on. Use the words as in the games described above.

2. Use a single die and tarot cards. Shuffle the cards and select 30 unseen. Deal face down into six adjacent piles of five. Throw

the die. The number thrown indicates the number of the pile from which to choose the first card. Throw and choose six times. Each card chosen reveals the next stage of the plot.

3. Dice are traditionally used for divination and insight. The meanings attributed to their scores can also be used in story-making (see next section).

Checklist
Use games of chance:

- to write a whole story

- to give your plot an unexpected twist

- to reveal new aspects of your characters

- when you are stuck.

Predictive and 'inner wisdom' techniques
The techniques described are ancient systems for attuning our-selves to archetypal energies and experiences, hence the term 'inner wisdom'. They can be used for divination, personal insight and guidance. Approached thoughtfully and with respect, they can also give insight into our characters and their stories.

Tarot spreads
The patterns in which the selected cards are laid are known as **spreads**. Many different spreads are described in the books and leaflets which accompany tarot packs. We can use these spreads to ask questions about our own lives and about the lives of our characters. The answers can also be read as an unfolding story.

'The Flying Bird' spread (Figure 5) works particularly well with the Osho Zen Tarot, which depicts concepts rather than characters. A recent Flying Bird spread read:

1. *Here and now*: turning inwards
2. *Resistance/fear*: participation
3. *Response to the fear*: stress
4. *Inner support*: healing
5. *External support*: innocence
6. *Relaxation/acceptance*: experiencing
7. *New awareness*: inner voice

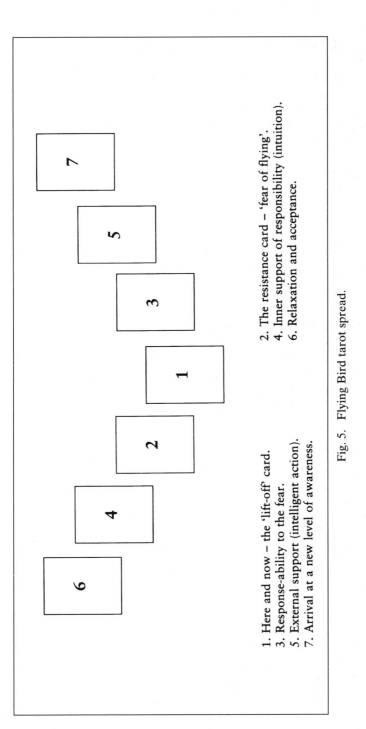

1. Here and now – the 'lift-off' card.
2. The resistance card – 'fear of flying'.
3. Response-ability to the fear.
4. Inner support of responsibility (intuition).
5. External support (intelligent action).
6. Relaxation and acceptance.
7. Arrival at a new level of awareness.

Fig. 5. Flying Bird tarot spread.

It gave rise to this story outline:

A woman in her forties has always wanted to dance (1) but is afraid of making a fool of herself (2). She finally psychs herself up to join a class, but when she gets there she feels unable to go in (3). A little girl (5) watching at the door tells her she longs to be in there dancing. The woman remembers feeling like that when she was young, and this gives her the courage she needs (4). Dancing at last, she feels positively euphoric (6). Later she tells the tutor how hard it was for her to take the first step. The tutor says 'I know – I saw you talking to yourself out there' (7).

The I Ching

This ancient Chinese system involves asking a question, throwing three coins six times to obtain a hexagram, and interpreting this by consulting the I Ching – or *Book of Changes* (available in numerous editions, translations and interpretations).

The answers are rich in metaphor. For instance, from Hexagram 59 HUAN: 'Clear what is blocking the light . . . Call a glass of water a pond if you like, but do not drown in it'; or from Hexagram 64 WEI CHI: 'A decisive new move . . . but not if you behave like the centipede who, looking at his moving feet and analysing their order of movement, ends up on his back waving his thousand legs in the air.'

The most useful answers result from sincere and well-formed questions. The answer to such questions, can reveal new aspects of a character, or change the plot dramatically. Many of the hexagrams offer a whole plot in themselves.

Runes

Norse in origin, each rune-stone bears an ancient alphabetical symbol. Bought sets include an accompanying booklet which gives the meaning of these. There are also many books on the subject available separately. Stones can be used singly or in spreads. As with the I Ching, answers can be interpreted in many ways. (The word 'riddle' – 'raedel' in Old English, comes from the Germanic 'raedan' or 'reading'.)

Some examples of runic food for thought are: from 1 The Self: 'Not a time to focus on results . . . look inside for the enemy of your progress' and from 5 Termination/New beginnings: 'In deep water become a diver'.

affected by their position in relation to each other and to areas of Cardinal, Fixed and Mutable energy.

Then there are 12 houses, representing the various stages of our journey through life and the way in which we interact with our environment. To borrow a phrase from psychology, the signs could be said to represent 'nature' and the houses 'nurture'. The appearance of planets in particular houses may either help or hinder our passage at that point.

Whatever our opinions regarding the validity of astrology, there is no doubt that it is a marvellous tool for writers. Once the basic principles are understood, we have only to choose a time, date and location for our character's birth – and endless possibilities for their development are revealed to us. We do not even have to face the laborious task of drawing up a chart, as there are numerous software packages which will do it for us (see Useful Addresses).

There are also specialised branches of astrology geared to specific purposes. Of particular interest to writers are:

1. **Age-point astrology** used by the Huber school (see Useful Addresses) charts significant periods in an individual's life.

2. **Horary astrology** answers questions by drawing up a chart for the moment when the question was posed (great for crime writers).

3. **Synastry** compares the chart of two individuals to discover the strengths and weaknesses of their relationship.

4. **Decumbiture** was used hundreds of years ago by physicians and herbalists to determine the best remedies to prescribe (useful for historical novelists).

5. **Astrocartography** advises on a choice of location, and the experiences we might have there at certain times.

Checklist
Astrology is an excellent tool for writers. It enables us to:

* know our characters thoroughly
* plot the course of a character's life

- answer questions on any aspect which puzzles us
- see how two characters might relate
- decide the best location for our story.

CASE STUDIES

Karen realises she has been 'talking to herself'

Karen has enjoyed writing in the privacy of her car and the garden shed, but feels her poetry is becoming too introspective. She wonders if others will understand it. When she wrote as a teenager – even in her diary – she imagined she was talking to someone of her own age. She has recently bought the Arthurian Tarot, and feels particularly drawn to the Grail Maiden. It is easy to imagine her as a receptive audience. She will try it.

David imagines his ex-boss as his audience

David's ex-boss was an absolute perfectionist. Nothing got past him, it seemed. David found this very irritating at the time, but admits he was motivated to do his best 'just to show him'. Imagining his boss as his audience is helping him to achieve similar standards in his writing. David also enjoys playing Scrabble and throwing dice to discover the next part of his story. Leaving the plot to chance seemed strange at first, but now he is hooked.

Sheila uses astrology to make her characters more convincing

Sheila has always been interested in astrology, but never thought of it as a writing tool. She has bought some astrological software, and finds it so effective in helping her to create rounded characters that she is thinking of enrolling in a correspondence course. First she will assess how much time this will take up, as she does not want to fall into her old pattern of distracting herself from her writing.

4

Develop Atmosphere, Pace and Mood

A good beginning grabs us, a skilful description engages our senses, a cleverly woven plot starts to intrigue us, we are warming to the characters – and then . . .

Think of some books you found all too easy to put down – that gathered dust beside the bed as you told yourself, 'I really must finish that'. What was missing? Is there one that satisfied most of the criteria at the beginning of this chapter, yet still failed to sustain your interest? Find it (if you have not thrown it away in frustration). Look at the first few chapters again. Having reacquainted yourself with it, how would you rate it in terms of:

- **Atmosphere** – the 'something in the air' that intrigues, excites, seduces, unsettles – 'draws you in'.

- **Pace** – is it crawling, cruising or speeding? Does it vary, or is it like a car with a stuck accelerator? Has the car broken down?

- **Mood** – in a sense, the 'inside-out' of atmosphere. Atmosphere affects a person's mood, and vice versa. How well does the author convey this?

If the author has got these right, you should feel 'part of the action'. You would probably have some physical reactions, however subtle: prickles of uneasiness at the back of the neck, excited flutters in the chest, stirrings in the gut, an 'oh *no*' somewhere in the throat. Chances are, this was what was missing when you gave up on the book in question.

Now choose a book that really got to you – one that had you propping up your eye-lids at 3 am because you just *had* to know what happened. Rate it on the same three aspects. How does it compare?

Think of a film or a TV drama that you would rate highly in this respect. Which were the most memorable scenes? What was it that made them so memorable? How do you feel physically as you recall them?

Think of a TV advertisement or a piece of 'on-the-spot' newspaper reporting which you would also rate highly in this way. How was this impact achieved?

We can benefit greatly from studying the way these three elements are handled in other media. Videos of successful screen drama are particularly useful for this purpose – even more so if you can obtain the script (see Useful Addresses).

Checklist
Skilful handling of atmosphere, pace and mood:

- draws you in

- makes you feel part of the action

- may be experienced physically

- is essential to a good read

- can be studied in a variety of media.

Choose a favourite video and novel to use as references as we work with each of these elements in turn.

CREATE AN ATMOSPHERE

A party with a really good atmosphere can 'take you out of yourself'. A party with no atmosphere has you casting surreptitious glances at your watch, wondering how soon is too soon to leave. It is the same with a story or a book. How do we create an atmosphere that makes people want to stay?

Find out how other writers do it
When writers are successful in creating atmosphere, they have probably immersed themselves in the setting (as discussed in Chapter 1). This is the first step. The following exercises look at the crafting of material generated in this way.

- What sort of atmosphere is created in the opening pages of your chosen book? Is it a general 'feel' for the setting, or does it evoke a specific response?

- What words, phrases and images does the author use to achieve this?

- What are the main vehicles the author uses for this purpose, eg colour, sound, other sense impressions, action, contrasts, character's response?

- Use these as headings to sort the author's words in note form. 'Chunk' the sections on the page (see Figure 1). This gives a clear overall picture, which offers considerable insight into the author's craft. It also makes the elements of that craft readily accessible as a stimulus for our own creativity.

- Repeat the exercise with some other favourite books.

- Repeat it with a favourite screen-drama video.

Use what you have learned

- Choose one page of notes from the previous section. Let your eye move at random around the chunks of words, until a particular phrase comes to the fore. Use it as the centre of a word web (see Figure 2).

- Let your eye move around the word web until a new phrase emerges. Create atmosphere through ten minutes of timed writing, starting with this phrase.

- In *one* word describe the atmosphere you created.

- Write a word that means the opposite.

- Brainstorm everything that comes to mind when you say that word.

- Sort and chunk your words as above.

- Use these notes to write a piece evoking this opposite atmosphere.

- Choose one of the pieces you have written. Tape yourself reading it. Use this as a guided visualisation to stimulate ideas.

More ways of working

Let the surroundings create the atmosphere
Let the surroundings tell their story. If the place we were in could speak, what would its voice be like? What would it say?
   Choose a tarot card which evokes the same atmosphere as you want to create. Let it represent your setting. Let it speak.

Imagine a soundtrack
What sort of music would go with this place? Close your eyes and imagine a soundtrack accompanying your opening scenes. Let your inner camera move around the location, focusing on different features and bringing some of them into close-up. Let the sound-track change and intensify as this occurs.

If you have a suitable piece of music, play it as you read your work aloud.

Work with a colour
For example, imagine something you own – or something connected with you in some way which is *red*. Allow it to become really vivid in your imagination. Make it *brighter*. Make it *bigger*. Imagine some stirring music to accompany this image. Make it *louder*. Imagine yourself in a crowd, dancing to this music in brilliant sunshine.

Play themed Scrabble
Sample themes: gothic, erotic, depressed, elated, Scandinavian, medieval, Monday morning, Christmas, airport, garden fête. Only words which evoke the atmosphere in question are allowed. Use them as suggested in Chapter 3.

Checklist
To develop a sense of atmosphere:

- immerse yourself in the setting of your story

- study the work of other writers

- let the surroundings speak

- imagine a soundtrack

- work with a colour

- play themed Scrabble.

SET THE PACE

Imagine your favourite piece of slow music played really fast, or vice versa. Worse, imagine all the music you ever listened to played at the same tempo throughout.

Getting the pace just right is extremely important. Handled properly it:

- enhances the atmosphere

- matches and underlines characters' moods

- advances or delays the action appropriately

- changes fairly frequently.

The last point can be a particular stumbling block. No matter how skilful the writing, too much delivered at the same speed can leave us feeling like a refugee from the January sales, or the recipient of a long sermon with no hard pew to keep us awake. Cinema and television with their ever shorter scenes and frequent changes of pace have no doubt influenced our tastes in this respect.

Study the structure
Watch your chosen video with the above criteria in mind.

- Pick some scenes where atmosphere is particularly important. What effect does the pace of those scenes have on their atmosphere?

- Note the way pace is matched to the main character's mood. Could this have been done differently?

- Select a 20-minute passage. Note the length and tempo of each scene within it. What is the proportion of fast to slow/short to longer scenes?

- Select a section of your chosen book to study in the same way.

Focus on the words
Camera movement, actors' performances and soundtrack all help to set the pace on screen. A novelist, journalist or storywriter has only words on paper through which to convey this vital element. Some writers come unstuck because they recall the fervour or languor with which they wrote, and therefore believe these have been committed to the page.

Masterly handling of pace leaves no doubt as to the author's intentions. Compare these extracts from Virginia Woolf's novel *The Waves*. Read them aloud several times as you study them.

First, the opening:

'The sun had not yet risen. The sea was indistinguishable from the sky, except that the sea was slightly creased as if a cloth had wrinkles in it. Gradually as the sky whitened a dark line lay on the horizon dividing the sea from the sky and the grey cloth became barred with thick strokes moving, one after another, beneath the surface, following each other, pursuing each other perpetually.'

The rhythm of this extract is like the in and out of the sea itself. It is almost impossible to read it any other way, or to hurry it. How is this achieved?

- Using this extract as a guide, create a descriptive piece with a similar tempo.

Later, the early morning sea is described:

'(The sun) bared its face and looked straight over the waves. They fell with a regular thud. They fell with the concussion of horses' hooves on the turf. Their sprays rose like the tossing of lances and assegais over the riders' heads. They swept the beach with steel blue and diamond-tipped water. They drew in and out with the energy, the muscularity, of an engine which sweeps its force in and out again.'

About half-way through the book, the afternoon sea is described:

'The waves massed themselves, curved their backs and crashed. Up spurted stones and shingle. They swept round the rocks, and the spray, leaping high, spattered the walls of a cave that had been dry before, and left pools inland, where some fish stranded lashed its tail as the wave drew back.'

The vitality of the images in the second two extracts defy us to read them meditatively – but that is just one element of the craftsmanship. You will have noticed the shorter sentences, and the way commas are used to break longer ones into short bites to hurry us along. (What might an inner-critic style English teacher say about commas between 'swept round the rocks, and the spray, leaping high', and none in the phrase 'where some fish stranded lashed its tail'?)

- Write a sequel to your first descriptive piece, using short sentences and 'unorthodox' commas to create urgency.

Use of the present participle ('ing' suffix) tends to slow down action. In the first extract there are four examples, in each of the others only one. The first extract uses only two images: the cloth and the lines, and these are introduced slowly. Description is mainly in the passive voice: 'the sea *was indistinguishable . . . was slightly creased*', 'the grey cloth *became barred*'. There is a dream-like detachment: '*as if a cloth had wrinkles in it*' rather than 'like a wrinkled cloth'. Later the sea becomes a cloth and, as in a dream, we do not question it.

- Read the first extract again. For the present participles, substitute 'which divided . . . which moved, followed, pursued'. Compare the effect.

- How many present participles did you use in your first descriptive piece? How much use did you make of the passive voice? Can you develop this further?

In complete contrast, the second and third extracts overflow with vigorously active images, which follow each other rapidly. In the second extract these are highly focused. Metaphorically, we are overtaken by the cavalry at full charge. We hear hooves, see weapons, riders – with 'the energy, the muscularity, of an engine'. In the third extract we are thrown from image to image: the waves, stones and shingle, rocks, spray, the walls of a cave. It feels like a performance of the 1812 Overture, complete with manic conductor in danger of being cut off by the tide.

- Develop your second descriptive piece further, introducing more images, using the active voice and limiting the use of present participles.

Focus on the sounds
Speech, like writing, is physical. Some sounds are less complex and easier to produce than others. 'M', one of the first consonants a baby learns to pronounce, is easy. So are 'B' and 'W'. They use natural lip positions. 'V', on the other hand, requires a tricky movement of the lower lip, and may be pronounced as 'W' in the early years. 'K' and 'G' require co-ordination of tongue and soft

palate. Short vowel sounds require least work from the larynx. Most can be 'grunted' with lips hanging loose: a – e – u – try it. Long vowels require more effort, and most diphthongs require this effort to be co-ordinated with tongue and lip movement.

Writers need to be aware of these relative complexities because the harder a sound is to make, the longer it takes to pronounce – and this affects pace. Even when we read silently, the brain carries on transmitting 'how to' messages to the body. Some people's lips move as they read. Most people's larynxes respond, however subtly.

- Experiment. Place your fingertips lightly on your Adam's apple and try some short vowel sounds followed by 'ou', 'oi', 'oo'. Try reading silently and notice any subtle movements of the larynx as you do so.

- Try all the consonants, noticing which ones require the most complex movements of the speech apparatus. (NB Those which require co-ordinated release of air – 'f', 'p' 'sh' etc are short sounds because they are explosive.)

- Read the Virginia Woolf extracts aloud in the light of these findings.

- Read a slow and a fast passage from your chosen book aloud, noticing what is happening to your speech apparatus as you do so.

Because we are accustomed to these physically imposed rhythms, we usually sort them naturally as we write. However, it is good to have them in mind when we analyse our work. 'Do I need more explosive consonants? Would longer vowel sounds work better here?' Such 'brush-strokes' can make all the difference.

Checklist
Pace is affected by:

- sentence length
- use of punctuation
- use of active or passive voice
- use of present participles

- number of images and their speed of presentation
- length of sounds involved in speaking the words.

GET INTO A MOOD

This title is chosen deliberately to express the fact that we cannot adequately convey a character's mood without experiencing it as we write. We can either start 'cold' and let the mood take us over as the words come together – or we can develop the mood within ourselves first and let the words flow from there. Many actors favour the latter approach, drawing on specific personal memories to help them portray emotion on stage. It is this approach that we will be using here, with the aid of guided visualisations.

Before starting, there is an important question to be considered. What do you do with this mood and these emotions afterwards? If the mood is a positive one, you may want to stay with it. If not, you will need to de-role. Sometimes you can do this by firmly stating your name (in other words stating that you are not the character you have been portraying). Turning to some familiar household task or talking to a friend can also help.

If the mood has taken over, you may need to repeat the visualisation that took you into it, substituting positive memories for oppressive ones. Revisiting difficult times takes courage, and should be avoided if currently under emotional stress.

Assuming you are not feeling fragile or that the mood you wish to explore is a positive one, the following visualisations should be taped and worked with in the usual way (see Chapter 2).

Guided visualisation 1: Mood sampling – energetic/tired

Close your eyes. Imagine yourself at the sea on a bracing day in early Summer. The sun is shining on the sea and it is also quite windy. The waves are crashing in. You can feel the wind whipping spray into your face.

Choose whether you want to go for a swim, or an invigorating walk along the front. Allow this image to fade.

Now turn your attention inwards – perhaps you are feeling a little tired just now – a little low in energy. So just let an image for that tiredness appear.

Let that image talk to you, and tell you how it feels . . . And what do you reply?

And now let an image for your energy appear . . . and let that
image talk to you . . . and what do you reply?
And now, become tiredness and talk to energy . . . And
switch roles – become energy and reply to tiredness.
Let this conversation between tiredness and energy continue
for a while. Switch roles whenever you need to. See what you
can discover.
When you are ready, open your eyes and make any notes you
need to make.

Guided visualisation 2: Recalling a mood

How is your character feeling at this point in the story? Can
you remember a time when you felt like this? Recall it in as
much detail as possible. Allow the feelings to increase in
intensity.
Where do you feel this most in your body?
Concentrate on this place in your body. Allow the feelings to
grow.
How big is this feeling now? What shape is it? What colour?
What kind of weather goes with this feeling? What temper-
ature?
What time of day goes with your feelings? What time of
year?
Think of a place that goes well with these feelings.
Allow an image of this place to develop. Explore it. Feel it.
Notice how it smells. What can you hear?
Notice objects the colour of your mood beginning to appear
in this place.
And now someone is approaching. They are dressed in this
colour.
They are carrying something which symbolises your mood.
Talk to them about it if you want to.
When you are ready, take your leave of this person. Return
to the present and make any notes you need to make.

- How are you feeling? Make this the subject of a timed writing.

- De-role if you need to.

Guided visualisation 3: Mood reflected in the environment

Return to the place you explored in visualisation 2. Give it a voice. Let it describe its feelings. How do you respond?

Search for the object which the person was carrying. Let it too have a voice and speak about its feelings . . . Let the object and place talk to one another. Is there anything you would like to say to them? Is any resolution needed? Who or what could help?

When whatever needs to be done is finished, return to the present and make any notes you need to make.

Writing practice

- Write for five minutes as the place, beginning 'I feel . . .'

- Write for five minutes as the object, beginning 'I feel . . .'

- Use both hands to write a dialogue between the two.

- What is the main feeling you have been exploring? Make it the centre of a web.

- Use the web to help you describe your character's mood.

- De-role if you need to.

Writing experiments

Using what you have discovered in this chapter, explore atmosphere and mood further by experimenting with different paces. Try:

- slow and fast: happiness, terror, supermarket

- a slow-motion rush hour

- inner turmoil/outer calm and vice versa.

Checklist

- A character's mood is likely to affect us as we write.

- We can reverse the process by evoking a mood and writing from it.

- It is unwise to evoke difficult emotions when we are under stress.

- We may need to de-role, and should know how to do this.

CASE STUDIES

Karen could not understand why she felt so 'down'

Karen could not explain a persistent feeling of sadness. When her boss spoke a bit abruptly one morning she burst into tears. A friend reminded her of the story she was writing about a troubled teenager. Karen's own teenage years were quite difficult. She now recognises how vulnerable she is in some areas, and is learning to take care of herself emotionally when she writes. She always de-roles now. She also asks the Grail Maiden to be her companion in visualisations.

David likes an analytical approach

David has enjoyed working analytically with a video of *Witness* and with his favourite crime novel. He feels he has learned a lot about setting the right pace – something which seemed to have eluded him before. He has become interested in how various sounds are formed, and is looking for a way to include this in a story. He has liked themed Scrabble and has used it to generate sinister and threatening words as well as words to do with police stations.

Sheila goes 'on location' with her binoculars

Sheila has been using binoculars for stargazing, and for a fresh look at the surrounding area. She has been imagining a sound-track for both. She has also taken photographs so that she can use a magnifying glass to re-create the tension and atmosphere at home. She feels this has brought her writing alive. She feels more confident about submitting her new radio play to the BBC, and hopes it will be favourably received.

5

Work with Beginnings and Endings

START WITH A BANG

There are beginnings that will not be ignored. Once read they stay with you, compel you to return, to read on.

Some are intriguing:

> 'Time is not a line but a dimension, like the dimensions of space. If you can bend space, you can bend time also, and if you knew enough and could move faster than light you could travel backwards in time and exist in two places at once.'
>
> (Margaret Atwood: *Cat's Eye*)

> 'As a baby, Tom Avery had twenty-seven mothers. So he says. Ask me more, his eyes beg, ask me for details.
> Well, then.'
>
> (Carol Shields: *Republic of Love*)

Some are bizarre or surreal:

> 'While Pearl Tull was dying, a funny thought occurred to her.'
>
> (Anne Tyler: *Dinner at the Homesick Restaurant*)

> 'You are about to begin reading Italo Calvino's new novel, *If on a winter's night a traveller*'.
>
> (Italo Calvino: *If on a winter's night a traveller*)

Some strike a chord deep within us:

> 'I exist! I am conceived to the chimes of midnight on the clock on the mantelpiece in the room across the hall.'
>
> (Kate Atkinson: *Behind the Scenes at the Museum*)

Some are shocking:

> 'All of us walk around naked. The delousing is finally over, and our striped suits are back from the tanks of Cyclone B solution, an efficient killer of lice in clothing, and of men in gas chambers.'
>
> (Tadeusz Borowski: *This Way for the Gas, Ladies and Gentlemen*)

Some plunge us into the middle of the action before we have time to think:

> 'He – for there could be no doubt of his sex, though the fashion of the time did something to disguise it – was in the act of slicing at the head of a Moor which swung from the rafters.
>
> (Virginia Woolf: *Orlando*)

or even into the middle of a conversation:

> ' "Yes, of course, if it's fine tomorrow," said Mrs Ramsay. "But you'll have to be up with the lark," she added.'
>
> (Virginia Woolf: *To the Lighthouse*)

The prize for the cleverest beginning ever should probably go to Adam Thorpe for the opening of *Still*. No more can be said about it without spoiling the impact. Experience it yourself if you have not done so already.

As well as hooking the reader's attention, the above beginnings serve another important purpose, ie revealing what kind of story this is going to be. In *How to Write a Million*, Orson Scott Card describes the opening paragraphs of a story as 'an implicit contract with the reader' whereby that reader 'knows what to expect, and holds the thread of that structure throughout the tale'. In each of the examples given, the expectations raised by the opening are fulfilled as the story unfolds (or not fulfilled in *To the Lighthouse* – the theme of which is unfulfilled expectations).

With just a few words, the authors caught their reader's attention and prepared the ground for everything that followed. How was this achieved?

Study a variety of beginnings

How did you react to those eight beginnings? Did they make you want to read on? Of those that did, can you say what it was about them that you liked or that impressed you? If you read on, did you feel that the author's 'implicit contract' with you was fulfilled?

- How would you answer the question 'What makes a good beginning?'

- Are there any differences between what makes a good beginning to a film, play or TV drama and what makes a good beginning to a story or novel?

Return to the book and video you studied in Chapter 4:

- Visualise the opening of the book as the start of a film.

- Write the opening of the video as the start of a book.

- Do these transpositions work? If not, why not?

Study opening scenes in both performed and written stories. Note what does and does not work for you. What changes would you make to the ones you find unsuccessful? Try some more transpositions from one medium to another.

Select the beginnings of five novels to use in the next section.

Use successful beginnings as a starting point

Brainstorm
Take each of your beginnings in turn. Write the first sentence. Spend five minutes brainstorming second sentences.

Do some timed writing
Use each of your beginnings and some of your brainstormed sentences as a stimulus for timed writing.

Start a new story
Take a favourite beginning and use it as the start of a new story. When the story is finished, go back and write your own beginning.

This is an excellent way to stop yourself agonising over your first paragraph. So is using any traditional opening: Once upon a time . . . Long ago in a far off land . . . There once lived . . . And it came to pass . . . Dearly beloved . . . There was this bloke, see? . . . Dear Mum . . . *anything* to get the words flowing onto the page. You can always change the beginning later.

Other starting points

Use the following as beginnings, then discard them – or not, as appropriate. Or use them as the inspiration which starts you off, without reproducing them on the page:

- an overheard remark

- a notice or headline

- a small ad in the local paper

- a proverb, or tongue-in-cheek version of a proverb

- a sentence picked from a book opened at random

- the first sentence you hear on turning on the TV or radio

- a line from a song.

ROUND THINGS OFF

What makes a good ending? Should it make you laugh – or cry – or think? This will depend on the genre, of course. It may make you shudder – as in *The October Game*, a story by Ray Bradbury in which the horrible truth dawns with the last sentence 'Then . . . some idiot turned on the lights'.

- What endings have you found particularly memorable?

- Would you rather end with action or reflection?

Some of the most satisfying endings bring the story full circle, like a piece of music returning to its original key. Good examples are the endings of two of the novels quoted in the first part of this chapter:

'And you say, "Just a moment, I've almost finished *If on a winter's night a traveller* by Italo Calvino."'
(Italo Calvino: *If on a winter's night a traveller*)

'I am alive. I am a precious jewel. I am a drop of blood. I am Ruby Lennox.'

(Kate Atkinson: *Behind the Scenes at the Museum*)

Some authors manage to sum up the whole story in a masterly final stroke. As does Anita Brookner in *Hotel du Lac*:

'. . . she wrote "Coming home". But, after a moment, she thought that this was not entirely accurate and, crossing out the words "Coming home," wrote simply, "Returning".'

Margaret Atwood, in *Cat's Eye* (see beginning of chapter) manages to bring the story full circle *and* sum it up in an extraordinarily poignant final paragraph:

'Now it's full night, clear, moonless and filled with stars, which are not eternal as was once thought, which are not where we think they are. If they were sounds, they would be echoes, of something that happened millions of years ago: a word made of numbers. Echoes of light, shining out of the midst of nothing.

It's old light, and there's not much of it. But it's enough to see by.'

Study endings

Return to the book and video you studied in Chapter 4. Study the endings of both. Do they fit any of the categories of ending mentioned above?

Transpose them, as before. Does this work?

Again, study performed and written work, this time focusing on endings. Note what works, what does not, and any changes that could be made. Try some more transpositions.

Select the final sentences of five novels to use in the next section.

Start at the end and work backwards

Brainstorm

Take each of your final sentences in turn. Spend five minutes brainstorming possible penultimate sentences for each one.

Do some timed writing
Use each of your final sentences and some of your brainstormed sentences as *the ending toward which your timed writing is heading*. (You are probably practised enough by now to sense when the buzzer is going to sound.)

Create a new story
Similarly, take a favourite beginning and write towards it to create a new story. When the story is finished, write your own ending.

Unfortunately traditional endings do not provide the same impetus as traditional beginnings: The End . . . That's all folks . . . Here endeth the lesson . . . Thank you and goodnight . . . RIP . . . Yours sincerely. These do not seem to have the same energy raising qualities. You may disagree.

FILL IN THE MIDDLE

Write each of the opening and closing sentences you have been studying on a separate strip of paper. Choose one of each unseen, and write for 15 minutes, creating a narrative which will join that beginning to that ending.

For example, using quotations from this chapter, you might choose as the first sentence: ' "Yes, of course, if it's fine tomorrow," said Mrs Ransay.' and as the last: 'Then . . . some idiot turned on the lights'. The task would be to write a story in between that made sense.

- Work your way through several pairings.

- Use the beginnings as endings and vice versa.

When you have finished, go through your narratives and highlight any ideas or phrases you could use in future. This is a good way to create the outline of a new story. Use some of the techniques from previous chapters to develop those narratives which show particular promise.

- Choose one of your narratives and develop it into a satisfying story.

- Pay particular attention to dialogue. How can this be used to move the story forward?

NB In the first instance use 'dummy dialogue', ie dialogue which conveys the required information, but is not yet crafted or personalised. This enables you to move ahead without interrupting the flow of ideas. Polish your dummy dialogue later.

Checklist

- Make your beginnings compelling.

- Make your endings provocative or satisfying.

- Improve your skills by studying the way beginnings and endings are handled in various media.

- Use existing beginnings and endings for inspiration and later discard them.

- Use 'dummy dialogue' in early drafts, so that the flow of ideas will not be interrupted.

Which usually comes first for you, a beginning, an ending, or a general idea?

CASE STUDIES

Karen's starting point is something she overheard

As Karen was queuing at the supermarket, she heard a man say, 'None of it would have happened if I hadn't left my glasses in the bed'. This set her imagination racing. Whose bed – and what was he doing in it that needed glasses? What chain of events was set in motion when he left them behind? How did he get them back? What did his wife say? She tackled these questions in her timed writing, and is using the results to write a collection of poems which she plans to call *I Spy*.

David uses the beginning of a best-seller to kick start his novel

David's redundancy money is not going to last as long as he hoped. Earning money from his writing suddenly feels like a priority. He decides to study some best-sellers and try to write in similar vein. With money very much on his mind he chooses Jeffrey Archer's *Not a Penny More, Not a Penny Less*, and laughs out loud in the shop when he reads the opening sentence, 'Making a million legally has always been difficult'. This is exactly the thought he needs to get started, and he finishes his first chapter surprisingly quickly.

Sheila gets an encouraging letter and does some research

Sheila is delighted to receive a letter from a producer who liked her play, but suggests a few changes. Sheila does not agree with all of them, but realises it would be in her interests to follow his advice at this stage. She studies his work by taping his latest play and buying tapes of others from the BBC. This gives her a good idea of his tastes and approach. She revises her play, resubmits it – and to keep her energies flowing, immediately starts work on the next one. She is putting astrology on the back burner for the moment.

6

Surprise Yourself

The activities in this chapter inject new energy into your work by introducing the unexpected.

WORK IN DEPTH

In the visualisations which follow, you will use objects of personal significance to help you work at a deeper level. Some of these objects will be used to 'time travel', rediscovering things you had forgotten. Some will be used to take you into new territory.

Use them to explore your own life first. Later, you can adapt the text of the visualisations to enable you to explore your characters' lives. This can be done in two ways:

1. On behalf of your character: you as author look at your character's life.
2. As your character: you become your character doing the visualisation.

Experiment to see which you prefer.

When you first do the visualisations, bear in mind the advice given in Chapter 4. Do not work too deeply if you are under emotional stress. One alternative is to visualise the scenes as though you were watching them on a stage or on television (see Visualisation 4). This helps you to feel less emotionally involved. Or it might be better to wait until you are feeling less vulnerable.

In Chapter 4, Karen asked the Grail Maiden to go with her on guided journeys. The Grail Maiden was acting as a **talisman** on those occasions. A talisman represents our own inner wisdom. It can be any person, animal or object which helps us to feel supported or protected. In guided journeys a talisman can also offer advice and answer questions. They are very useful to have with us.

Close your eyes for a moment and allow a talisman to appear for you. Ask this talisman to accompany you in these visualisations.

NB As these visualisations work at a deeper level, when you tape them allow longer pauses than before, giving your imagination plenty of time to explore.

Visualisation 1: Backpack (useful when starting a new story)

You are about to start a journey. Will you journey by day or by night?

When you have decided, find yourself in a meadow, with your talisman. Somewhere nearby is the road or path which will start you on your journey – but you need not concern yourself with that at the moment. Sit down in the meadow and rest for a while.

You have with you a backpack. In it is everything you will need for this journey. What is this backpack like? How big is it? What colour? What shape?

Open it now. See all the things inside it. Take them out one by one and lay them on the grass. Spend some time looking at all these things which were in your backpack. You may want to discuss them with your talisman.

(allow at least two minutes pause here)

And now it is time to leave the meadow and begin your journey. How will you travel? On foot, or by some other means?

When you have chosen your means of travel, you see that there are three paths ahead of you – one to the right, one to the left, and another straight ahead. Your talisman helps you choose the path to take, and you begin your journey.

What sort of landscape are you passing through?

Are there any trees, or other vegetation? Are there any people along the way? Any animals?

Do you need anything from your backpack at this stage?

And now you see that there is an obstacle in your path. Is there anything in your backpack which will help you deal with it? You may need to ask the talisman to help you decide what to do.

When you have dealt with the obstacle continue your journey.

And now you encounter another obstacle . . . and with the aid of the things in your backpack you deal with it successfully.

And now you see that you are approaching a mountainous

---

region, and there is a mountain which you are going to climb
. . . and there is something in your backpack which will help
you to do this in an ingenious way, which you have never
tried before. It is amazingly easy . . . and before long you
have reached the top. Stand looking down at the path
you have taken. You can see the two obstacles down there
looking very small.

Talk with your talisman about other ways you might have
dealt with them.

And now it is time to return, so make your way back down
the mountain.

And make your way back to the meadow.

Spend a little time in the meadow reflecting on your journey,
and the ways in which the things in your backpack helped
you. Thank the talisman and any other beings which
helped you on your journey.

When you are ready, open your eyes and make any notes you
need to make.

- Use this journey as the subject of a 20-minute timed
  writing.

Use the talisman in your own way in the next three visualisations.

Visualisation 2: Toy box (revisiting childhood)

Close your eyes – and find yourself in the bedroom you had
as a child.

How old are you?

Spend some time rediscovering this room – the bed . . . the
bed covers . . . the furniture . . . the curtains . . . the wallpaper
. . . the floor coverings.

And in a corner of the room, out of sight, you now see a big
toy box.

And in that toy box are all the toys that belong to you. Open
it, and spend some time now looking at all your toys.

(allow at least two minutes)

Choose a favourite toy now. Hold it, feel it. What does it
smell like?

Let that toy take you to a time when you especially remember playing with it, or having it with you. Take a few
moments to experience that time again.

When you are ready, choose another toy and let it help you
to remember.

Choose as many toys as you want to – until you feel ready to
close the toy box and return to the present.

When you are ready, open your eyes and make any notes you
need to make.

Visualisation 3: Wardrobe (revisiting your teens)

Close your eyes – and find yourself in the bedroom you had
as a teenager.

Spend some time getting to know that bedroom again.

And now you particularly notice that at one side of the room
is a huge wardrobe – it may be one you remember, or it may
be much bigger.

And inside it are all the clothes you wore as a teenager, at
home, at school, for different activities . . . Open the wardrobe now, and take some time to get to know those clothes
again.

(long pause)

And now, choose one particular garment or outfit. Take it
out. Hold it against you. Hold it away from you and look at
it carefully. What does the material feel like? What does it
smell like?

Now remember what it was like to wear it. Remember yourself dressed in it. How does that feel?

Let this garment or outfit take you to a time when you were
wearing it. Remember what happened.

Try as many different outfits as you want to – until you feel
ready to put them away again, close the wardrobe and return
to the present.

Make any notes you need to make.

(You may like to visit other decades of your life in this way)

• What will you do with these memories? They can be used
  in timed writing or a story, or to help explain something in
  your life that has puzzled you. You could also make the
  name of a toy or a garment the centre of a web.

Visualisation 4: Theatre of life (looking at a significant event)

Close your eyes – and imagine you are in a theatre. The curtain is down. The play will be beginning soon. This is to be a private showing just for you – and perhaps a few friends if you want them there.

The play is about a significant happening in your life. It will be in three acts: Act 1 will show the events leading up to it; Act 2 will show the happening itself; Act 3 will show the results of that happening.

Who will be in the cast? Where will these different acts be taking place?

And now, the lights dim in the theatre . . . the curtains open . . . you see the scene – and the characters . . . and Act 1 begins. Watch now as the events which lead up to that significant happening begin to unfold.

(pause for at least two minutes)

And now it is time for the curtain to come down on Act 1. You may go backstage and talk to the actors if you want to, or you may stay in your seat and think or talk about what you have seen.

And now it is time for Act 2 to begin. The lights dim . . . the curtains open. What is happening? Watch as this significant happening in your life unfolds.

(pause for at least two minutes)

And now it is time for the curtain to come down on Act 2 – is there anything you need to do before Act 3?

And now it is time for Act 3 to begin. The lights dim . . . the curtains open . . . and you can see the results of what happened in Act 2 begin to unfold. How do you feel as you watch this story being told?

(pause for at least two minutes)

And now it is time for the curtain to come down on Act 3. How are you feeling at the end of the play?

Is there anything you would like to change – any scenes you would like to rewrite? If so, in which act or acts did these scenes appear?

You are invited to go up onto the stage now and appear in these rewritten scenes. You can play either yourself or one of the other characters. You can appear in as many scenes as you wish, in as many parts as you wish.

Continue until you have acted out all the changes you want to make.

(pause for as long as required)

As you come to the end of your changes, you notice that the auditorium is now full of people. You walk to the front of the stage and take a bow as the audience claps and cheers. Your new play is a definite hit.

When you are ready, allow the curtain to come down and the lights to dim. Say anything you need to say to the rest of the cast, and take your leave of them. Return to the present, open your eyes and make any notes you need to make.

- You might like to record this experience in the form of a play.

PLAY WITH WORDS AND IMAGES

Consequences (two group activities for 4–6 people)

Activity 1: Sending your character out into the world
Each person will need a sheet of paper (preferably A3) and a pen. Fold the paper into 12 sections (in half, in half again, then in thirds).

- Think of a character you are working with at present – or invent a new one.

- In the first section, draw your character in a scene from your story.

- Pass your paper to the left. Take some time to absorb the picture you have received, then draw what happens next in the next section.

- Continue passing to the left and drawing what happens next, until all 11 sections have been filled.

- In the twelfth section write the conclusion of the story.

- Retrieve your original paper and study the story which has now evolved.

- Take 15 minutes to write it.

- Read your stories to the rest of the group.

In the first part of that activity, you acted out symbolically what a writer does. You invented something and passed it on for other people to interpret in their own way. Our work is only partly our invention once it has gone out into the world. Then it also becomes part of other people's creative process.

- How did it feel to let your character pass out of your hands?

- How did you feel when you saw what had happened to your character?

Activity 2: Creating a bizarre situation
Each person will need a sheet of paper and a pen.

- At the top of your sheet of paper write an adjective. Fold it over once so that the word is hidden. Pass it to the left.

- On the paper you received, write a noun. Fold as before and pass it on.

- Now write a verb in the past tense. Fold and pass it on.

- Now write a preposition. Fold, pass it on.

- Write an adjective. Fold, pass it on.

- Write a noun. Fold, pass it on.

- Unfold the sheets of paper and read out the sentences that have been made, inserting *a, an, the* where necessary.

Use some or all of these, probably bizarre, sentences in any way you choose.

Random words (group or solo activity)
You will need paper cut into ten strips, and a volunteer (if working in a group) to act as reader.
   Choose a beginning and an ending from different stories. Or choose two sentences at random. Use one as a beginning, one as an ending. The task is to write narrative that will join one to the other, as in Chapter 5 – *but with a difference.*

- If in a group, divide the strips of paper among them. One word is to be written on each strip and passed to the reader. If working alone, open the dictionary, point to a word and write it on a strip. Repeat ten times.

- Begin writing. As you write, the reader will select a strip and read the word on it aloud (or you will select your own strip if working alone). The word must be incorporated into your writing within the next sentence or two.

- Continue until all the strips are used up.

Instead of writing words on strips you can use a radio, turning up the volume from time to time and using the first word you hear. This can also liven up your daily timed writing.

Reversals

Clichés can be revitalised by turning them around. For example:

- 'Work is the curse of the drinking classes' (Oscar Wilde).

- 'My senses were taking leave of me' (Christine Miller, poet).

- Overheard in a pub: 'The young people of today don't know how to have a punch-up without enjoying themselves.'

We can also reverse frequently used phrases. A person with a strict upbringing might say: 'Other people's parents ran to meet them – mine met to run me'.

Describing a wimp we might say 'he never chanced a stand'.

A poet distracted by love might describe his beloved's voice as 'Music to his ears, but earache to his muse'.

Someone whose house needs rewiring might have 'too many fires in the iron'.

There is also some mileage in reversing initial consonants (Spoonerisms). For example, of a character who frequently burns food, we could say 'Everything is mist to his grill'.

Checklist

Surprise yourself into writing by:

- exploring the past in guided journeys

- creating group stories

- injecting random words into your writing

- using reversals.

CASE STUDIES

Karen uses her slips of the tongue
Karen sometimes gets her words muddled, especially when she is tired. She used to be embarrassed about it, but now she often makes a note of things she says by accident. She has used these Spoonerisms in her *I Spy* collection, which is becoming increasingly humorous – a new departure for Karen.

David enjoys thinking up reversals
Reversals really appeal to David's sense of humour. He has thought up dozens and is thinking of sending the best ones to a greetings card company. He is also working at turning some of them into jokes for *Week Ending* and similar programmes, which might make him some money. It is proving more difficult than he thought.

Sheila uncovers some early memories
Sheila was surprised at the power of the images and feelings evoked by the toy box visualisation. It was like being three or four years old again. She has used some of these long forgotten memories as flashbacks for a character in her new play. She is excited by the authenticity this approach brings to her writing.

7

Work with your Dreams

A DIFFERENT WORLD

In ancient times, dreams were thought to be sent by the gods. When we work with them, it is easy to understand why. Dreams are wondrous, mysterious. They offer messages and gifts. They take us into a different world, with different rules – a magical world that is likely to vanish like Cinderella's finery if we so much as clean our teeth before writing down what we experienced there.

In this chapter we will learn how to enter that world with awareness and bring its treasures back to use in the waking world.

It would be useful to start with a very brief introduction to the pioneering work done by the Austrian psychoanalyst, Sigmund Freud and his Swiss contemporary Carl Jung in this respect.

Freud and dreams
Sigmund Freud had enormous respect for dreams, and considered his book *The Interpretation of Dreams* to be his most important work. The hundreds of dreams transcribed in it make it a rich resource for writers.

Freud's studies confirmed his view that nothing we have experienced is ever fully lost to us. Events which are inaccessible to conscious memory remain in a vast subconscious store which can be tapped through dreams and visualisation. Even the most trivial details are retrievable: 'the wart on the forehead of a stranger' as he puts it. These are truly 'gifts from the gods' to a writer. That wart might be the very thing that wins the Booker Prize!

Jung and dreams
Carl Jung also placed great emphasis on dreams. In the second half of his book *Dreams* he relates individual dream symbols to mythology and alchemy. Again, this is a rich resource for writers.

Jung gave us the theory explored earlier in relation to visualisation – that all elements of the dream represent aspects of the dreamer's personality. We will be looking at a number of ways of working with this later in the chapter.

In order to open himself fully to what a dream had to offer, Jung would start from the premise 'I have no idea what this means'. To get to the heart of the image and extract its full meaning, Jung would say to his client 'Suppose I knew nothing at all about a . . . Describe it to me in the greatest possible detail'.

This open approach is yet another way in which we can surprise ourselves rather than limit our possibilities to what we 'know'.

USING DREAM EXPERIENCES

Keep a dream journal

Why record dreams?
The fact that dreams are so often forgotten on waking was one of the reasons Jung urged his clients to write them down straight away (an idea which seems obvious now, but was regarded as rather odd at the time). Another reason for recommending the regular recording of dreams was his interest in dream series. Keeping a journal helps us to recognise patterns and identify themes in our dreams – useful both for personal work and in using our dreams for story making.

Particularly significant on both counts is Jung's discovery that when we work with a series of dreams, *later ones often correct mistakes we make in working on earlier ones*. This is a dramatic illustration of the interactive process which occurs when we give dreams our full attention. The very act of keeping a special book, and recording our dreams thoughtfully in it, lets the psyche know that we are serious, and the psyche responds accordingly.

How should dreams be recorded?
Most therapists who work with dreams ask that they be related in the present tense. This reconnects the dreamer with the energies of the experience, and makes the work far more powerful. The same principle applies when we use dreams in story making. Recording them in the present tense puts us in touch with the energies and gives the work immediacy. Reading them aloud can also be helpful. Taping this reading and playing it back to yourself can be very powerful.

- While the dream is still fresh in your memory, ask: 'If this were a film, what would its title be?' Record this title and your reasons for choosing it.

- Are there any changes you would like to make to this dream? If there are, record them.

- Ask 'What happened next?' and continue your dream in the form of a visualisation. Or ask 'What was happening just before the point where my dream began?' Record your answers.

Some people claim they never dream. In fact everybody dreams at regular intervals throughout their sleep time, but the dreams are not always remembered. We can change this by actively encouraging the process, as described further on in this chapter.

American dreamwork therapist Strephon Kaplan-Williams recommends recording your thoughts on waking each day, whether you remember any dreams or not. Like timed writing, this maintains the momentum of the process.

The way in which you choose to organise your dream journal is a personal matter. You might record in a linear way or in chunks, chronologically or under themes. You might draw pictures, include cuttings, use coloured pens etc.

A method I have found particularly useful for identifying patterns and themes is the use of an A4 page-a-day any-year diary. In this I record dreams and, very briefly, significant daily events. This takes at the most 15 lines. There are 52 lines to a page. At the end of the year I start again at 1 January, writing under the previous entry. By the third or fourth time round, patterns are very clear. The two-line days tend to be two-liners every year. The 15-liners may expand.

Aggravation with the car tends to recur within a few days either side of the previous anniversary. The computer crashes on the same evening as it did two years ago – and the dreams with certain themes tend to have their special times of year to recur as well. It is a weird and enlightening experience.

Checklist
Dreams:

- may be capable of putting us in touch with everything we have experienced

- may represent many aspects of the dreamer's personality

- are best approached in a state of not knowing

- may be forgotten if not recorded straight away

- sometimes occur in series, and these can be self-regulating

- are best related in the present tense

- occur at regular intervals during sleep, but are not always remembered.

Working with dream images

Les Peto, author of *The Dream Lover*, compares dreams to the intensely real world of play in childhood. Like Jung, he recommends a wondering, childlike approach in working with them. He describes dreams as 'feeling-pictures – almost entirely silent movies, which rely for their impact on striking visual images, larger than life, surreal and irrational situations'.

He suggests listing all the images, then taking each one and saying 'This reminds me of . . .', writing down everything that comes, even if it seems silly.

- For a different perspective try drawing each image instead of listing them.

- Visualise yourself as all the different parts (as you did in Chapter 3), characters, furniture, the building or landscape you are in – everything. What do they have to say? How do they see you, the dreamer?

Working with one incident

Draw what happened
Recall a specific incident from a dream. Who are all the people involved? Where are they standing? Where are all the objects placed? What are the surroundings like? Draw the incident, making the drawing as detailed as you can. It will be like a snapshot or a still from a film.

- Using the present tense, describe exactly what you see.

- Describe the scene from the point of view of each person or thing you drew.

Show what happened
As above, but this time the scene is acted out, either in person or using objects to represent all the elements of the dream.

Take it on
After you have drawn or acted out your scene, draw, act or write the next scene.

Take it back
Draw, act or write what was happening just before that scene.

What is missing?
Sometimes who or what is missing can give insight: 'I am looking for my glasses'. 'It was mid-day and the postman had not come.' So – what would you have been able to see if you had your glasses? What would the postman have brought? Or – what has happened to the postman on the way to your house?

Exploring the mood of a dream
Spend some time getting in touch with the dream again. What do you feel as you remember it? Do you have an image for that feeling? What shape is it? Does it have a colour? Where do you experience it in your body? Does it have a voice? What kind of voice? What does it say? Focus on the feeling again. What would the opposite of that feeling be? Work with the opposite feeling in the same way.

Working with the body language
Gestalt therapy pioneer Fritz Perls felt that the message of a dream was best discovered freshly from within the self, not from an external interpretation. He would often work with the body language a person used as they related their dream. Some of the techniques he developed were:

- *Do it more* – make the gesture bigger, faster. Make that sound more loudly. This might help us to get the message the dream is trying to convey.

- *Do the opposite* – how does that feel?

- *Finish what you started* – finish the kick, punch, caress, choked off scream etc.

What sort of dream is it?

The methods looked at so far will help you to get every last gram of value from your dream images. It is also helpful to know what kind of dream you are dealing with. In his book *Elements of Dreamwork*, Strephon Kaplan-Williams lists 24 major dream types. They include dreams which:

- reflect unresolved issues from childhood

- confirm the validity of our waking-life actions

- enable us to experience things not possible in waking life

- present issues to be worked through and resolved

- reveal accurately the dynamics of a close relationship.

Checklist

To get the most from your dreamwork:

- explore every image

- explore a single 'snap-shot' incidents

- explore the feelings

- work with the body language

- think about what kind of dream you have had.

AWARE DREAMING

To encourage aware dreaming (and relieve insomnia) set up an internal dream sanctuary. Furnish it with things conducive to peaceful sleep: scented oils, soft lighting, music or silence according to your preference. Imagine the softest of beds – perhaps a fluffy cloud which gently rocks. Spend some time imagining this sanctuary in every detail, so you can go straight there when you close your eyes.

The process can also be encouraged by music designed to slow the brainwaves – such as the Delta Sync Sleep System CDs from LifeTools. Again, the *intention* to engage with your dreams is conveyed to the psyche because you have backed it up with appropriate action. The psyche will respond. Affirm your intention verbally, repeating a phrase such as 'Tonight I will remember my dreams'. Strengthen this affirmation by writing it down. Place a hand on your chest or abdomen and experience its weight and warmth. This helps to anchor your affirmation further. Don't be discouraged if results are not immediate. The most effective strategy is calm persistence. It will bring results eventually.

The next step is to indicate *what* it is you would like to dream about and remember. Answers to questions and solutions to problems can be sought. Include written and verbal questions about your writing. With practice you can dream about your characters. Sometimes the next chapter or story gets acted out more or less in total – an amazing experience. There are hypnotic suggestion tapes designed to achieve this level of engagement with dreams. I recommend Dick Sutphen's *Dream Solutions* and Paul Sheele's *Programming Your Dreams*, available from New World Music and LifeTools respectively.

However, to reiterate, the most effective technique by far is *perseverance.*

Lucid dreaming

Lucid, or conscious dreaming takes the process a stage further by enabling those who practise it to know they are dreaming. The dream can be manipulated to suit specific purposes. For example, you could get the characters of your story or novel together and direct them in a specific scene.

It takes dedicated practice to achieve this degree of facility. There are special exercises designed for the purpose. There are also devices, such as sleep masks which respond to the rapid movements made by the eyes when we are dreaming. A buzzer is activated which, eventually, is perceived by the dreaming mind and recognised as a signal that dreaming is taking place. Further information about this, and about lucid dreaming in general, can be obtained from LifeTools.

Opinion is divided as to the merits of lucid dreaming. Some see it as a tool for inner discovery, others feel that conscious intervention interferes with the processes of the subconscious.

Checklist

We can learn to interact more fully with our dreams by:

- setting up an internal dream sanctuary

- making our intentions clear

- choosing the way that is right for us

- *persevering*.

CASE STUDIES

Karen dreams about the Grail Maiden
Karen had been going through a stressful period and this had affected her sleep patterns. She had not remembered any dreams for a long time. She started to work on an internal dream sanctuary, and also bought some sleep-inducing tapes. She slept soundly the first night she tried them, but remembered no dreams. The second night she spent time affirming an intention to remember her dreams. She dreamed of the Grail Maiden, and woke up feeling extremely calm.

David tries to dream lucidly
The idea of lucid dreaming appealed greatly to David. He bought a book on the subject and tried the exercises nightly for nearly three weeks before he started getting results. However, he has found his lucid dreams quite boring. The stories his characters acted out were less interesting than those he has arrived at by other means, such as timed writing and themed Scrabble. He is beginning to agree with the view that it interferes with the workings of the subconscious.

Sheila finds a pattern in her dreams
Sheila has been keeping a dream journal regularly for over a year now, and is beginning to notice certain themes recurring. She is also noticing that high and low levels of dream activity tend to go in cycles. She can now wait calmly for the next high activity period, and not panic when her dreams seem to have disappeared. She has also reached the stage where she can get her writing questions answered during those active periods, and this is proving very helpful.

8

Recycling

Sometimes a new character, setting or plot just comes to us. We wake up with a brilliant idea. We see or hear something that kick-starts our imagination.

When this is not the case try revamping 'one you made earlier'. Or revamp one that somebody else made – rather in the spirit of George Washington's axe. ('This is the very axe George Washington used when he chopped down the cherry tree,' the proud owner tells his visitors. 'Of course, it's had four new handles and three new heads since then.')

Amazing what a new head will do.

GIVE OLD CHARACTERS A MAKEOVER

Change one aspect
A single change can radically affect the whole picture. Other features become incongruous or find themselves in direct conflict with the newcomer. They have to adapt – or fight.

Imagine: Henry the Eighth as a woman, Tina Turner as a village post-mistress, Ophelia in a bikini, Gandhi as West Indian.

Take any familiar character and try changing their:

- gender

- age

- nationality

- social status

- historical period

- occupation

- state of health

- style of dress

- marital/family status

- sexual orientation

- religion

- politics

- geographical location

- planet.

Changing one aspect is a very useful way of developing a character who is based on somebody you know – particularly yourself. It creates some distance, which enables you to see new possibilities.

Change a few aspects
Try the exercise again, changing two or three of the aspects. What effect did this have? How much of your original character remains?

Change everything
In the last chapter we experienced the effect of working with opposites. We can use this technique to invent someone who is the exact opposite of our original character (and probably represents their hidden self).

This new character can be used in their own story, or placed in conflict with the original, as in Robert Louis Stevenson's *Strange Case of Dr Jekyll and Mr Hyde*.

Visualising opposites
Use this short visualisation to experience opposites, focusing first on yourself.

Close your eyes. Become aware of yourself, your qualities, your feelings . . . Think of three adjectives that you would use to describe your own character – the essence of you . . . take your time . . .

Now think of the *opposites* of those words. Become a person who has those opposite characteristics . . . what are you like now?

How does it feel to be this person? . . . What is your life like? . . .
What do you dislike about being this person? . . . What do you like? . . .
Take a little time to really get in touch with what it is like to be this person. Now become yourself again. Open your eyes. Say your name out loud. Make any notes you need to make.

- Make the comparison of these two experiences a subject for timed writing.
- Write a dialogue for yourself and your 'opposite self'.
- Repeat the exercise as a character in one of your stories.

Create the complete opposite
Choose a familiar character and brainstorm all the things you know about them. Now write the opposite of each characteristic you have listed, thus creating a completely new character.

- Get to know this character by using the tuning in exercises and visualisations from Chapter 2.

- Ask them to tell you their story.

- Write a scene where the original character and the opposite character meet each other.

GIVE OLD SETTINGS A FACELIFT

Changing the setting in this way is particularly useful when the subject matter of a story relates closely to something in our personal life. The setting where the original event took place might be so firmly fixed in our mind that we get bogged down. Making even a minor change can enable us to move on.

Minor alterations

- Visualise your setting at different times of year, different times of day, different days of the week, in all possible weathers, in a different era.

- Use each visualisation as the subject of timed writing.

- Build a new house, school or supermarket there.

- Make a certain colour predominant.

- Fill the place with people.

- Empty it of people.

- Ask the setting how it responds to these changes.

Major rebuilding

- Brainstorm all the characteristics of the place. Write their opposites and use these to create a new setting.

- Transfer both settings from inland to the coast, or vice versa.

- Build a motorway beside one of them.

- Transfer one to the top of a mountain.

- Make one a tourist attraction because of its . . . ?

- Build a new housing development or a factory.

- Visualise the aftermath of a disaster.

- Pull down buildings or put up new ones.

- Build a tunnel or a bridge.

- Employ an avant-garde architect to make his or her mark on the environment.

Choose one or two of these major changes, and write as the setting, or as the change – or put the setting and the change in dialogue with each other. Make these personalisations the subject of timed writing.

Checklist
Create new characters and settings from old ones by:

- changing one major or minor aspect

- changing a few aspects

- creating the exact opposite.

NEW PLOTS FROM OLD

Branching narratives – simple version

Choose a familiar story or novel of the genre in which you would like to write. Break down the plot into its most basic steps. To take a very simple example, the story of Little Red Riding Hood can be broken down into these six steps:

1. Red Riding Hood sets out to visit her grandmother, who is ill.

2. A wolf tricks her into revealing where her grandmother lives.

3. The wolf goes ahead of her and eats grandmother.

4. When Red Riding Hood arrives, the wolf tricks her by pretending to be her grandmother.

5. The wolf eats Red Riding Hood.

6. Her father kills the wolf, cuts it open and frees Red Riding Hood and grandmother.

When you have broken down the plot of your story in this way, invent an alternative for each of the steps from 2 onwards. For example, in Little Red Riding Hood, step 2(a) could be *She loses her way and ends up at a house she has never seen before* – which would take the story along an entirely different route. Or, keeping the original step 2, step 3(a) could be *the wolf is a DSS inspector in disguise*. As with changing one aspect of a character, the original is radically altered from the point at which you intervene.

If you were following this procedure for real, rather than as an exercise, you would also disguise the basic details in the steps prior to your intervention. For example, intervene at step 3 in Little Red Riding Hood, keeping the gist of 1 and 2 the same, but making the main character a little boy in a blue anorak on his way to see a friend. Have a woman trick him into revealing his friend's address.

Or, having intervened at step 3 and finished the story, write backwards from 3, inventing an alternative step 2 and a new beginning.

Or work backwards from either the old or new beginning – as in dreamwork when you asked what was happening before the dream began. What were the events in the life of Red Riding Hood or the boy in the anorak, which led them to set out alone that morning? A whole family saga could be awaiting revelation.

After you have made your alterations, the finished product will be unrecognisable in terms of the original – a real George Washington's axe-job.

Many short stories in women's magazines can be broken down and used as templates in this way (and many were probably devised in a similar way to begin with). Most of these have a fairly simple plot which would fit the six-step model. Some stories are more complex than they might at first appear: Cinderella for example takes roughly 13 steps:

1. Cinderella's stepmother and her two daughters are jealous of Cinderella's beauty and treat her as a servant.

2. They receive an invitation to the ball the king is giving for his son, and are determined that Cinderella shall not go.

3. When they have left for the ball, Cinderella's fairy godmother changes her rags into a satin gown and glass slippers, and turns a pumpkin into a coach.

4. She sends Cinderella off to the ball, warning her to be home by midnight, when the spell will wear off.

5. The prince falls in love with Cinderella and dances with her all evening.

6. Midnight strikes. Cinderella remembers the warning and flees in panic.

7. Everything changes back except the glass slippers. One is left behind.

8. The prince orders every woman in the land to try the slipper, and vows to marry the one it fits.

9. The sisters lock Cinderella up while they try the slipper. Their feet are too big.

10. Just as the prince's entourage is leaving, Cinderella escapes.

11. She tries the slipper and it fits. She also has the other one.

12. Cinderella marries the prince.

13. They live happily ever after.

(*War and Peace* is not recommended as a candidate for this treatment!)

Simple branching narrative visualisation

Choose a beginning sentence. Write this sentence and then close your eyes.

Where does this first sentence take you? Take some time to get in touch with your surroundings.

Who are you? Take some time to get to know this character whose life you have stepped into.

There is a problem on your mind. What is it? Open your eyes long enough to write what it is.

This is the first place where your story branches. There are two things you could do about this problem. What are they?

When you are ready, open your eyes and write these two solutions side by side. Close your eyes again.

Choose one of these solutions. Picture yourself carrying it out. Picture this in great detail.

Suddenly another person appears. Because they are here, two things could happen next. What are they?

Open your eyes long enough to write these two possibilities side by side.

Choose one of the possibilities. Picture it taking place. Picture this in great detail.

Something is about to occur now, which will take you on towards the end of your story. What is it? As you think about it, maybe other possibilities will present themselves.

Open your eyes and write down these possibilities as they occur to you.

Close your eyes and choose one of the possibilities. Picture it happening.

Choose two possible endings. Open your eyes and write these two endings.

Simple branching narrative with added complication

If the vehicle is a short story, it would be best to limit yourself to between 13 and 15 steps along the path of one person's fortunes. If working with a longer form, however, we could, at any point in the original or altered narrative, introduce a new element which would take the story off on a different route – result in a sub-plot, a lengthening of the original plot, the rise to prominence of a second character, or a completely new direction.

For example, after step 5, *The prince falls in love with Cinderella and dances with her all evening*, we could insert *A messenger arrives from . . . Enemy troops are gathering. The prince must lead the army into battle to defend the kingdom.*

With no prince to defend her, Cinderella might be arrested after step 6 and languish in a dungeon until his return. Meanwhile we diverge from the main plot in order to follow the prince into battle.

Branching narratives – complex version

In this version every alternative step generates two possible next steps, building up a narrative tree as in Figure 6.

Italo Calvino's story *The Count of Monte Cristo* is a branching narrative in which all branches are presented for consideration.

Other story-making methods

The question game

Sometimes known as 'I had a dream', this game requires a partner. The partner questions you about your story/dream in terms that require a yes or no answer. Your response affects subsequent questions and a story gradually emerges.

The rule, unknown to the questioner, is that a question ending with the letter 'e' is answered with 'yes'. All others are answered 'no'.

Plot-generating software

These are electronic versions of the branching narrative idea and range from the simple and inexpensive, such as 'Plotpro', to more sophisticated models costing several hundred pounds. See Useful Addresses – and *ask for a demonstration* in order to be sure the programme suits your particular needs and style.

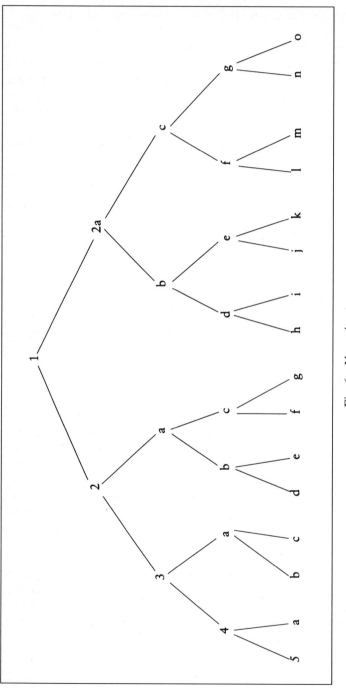

Fig. 6. Narrative tree.

NEW TEXT FROM OLD

'S + 7'

This is a method which originated with a group of French experimental novelists. The 'S' may stand for *sujet* (subject). Sometimes it generates ideas for plots. More often it produces new modes of expression – phrases unlikely to have arisen from logical thought. Many people find it positively addictive.

You will need a small, very basic dictionary. The English section of a foreign language translating dictionary is ideal.

The method

Take any text. Begin to copy it. Each time you come to a noun, find it in the dictionary, count forward seven words and use that word instead.

If the word you arrive at is not a noun, change it to a noun. If this is not possible, move to the next noun.

Alternatives

Change verbs and/or adjectives as well. Count a different number of words. Count backwards instead of forwards. Use nearby words if you prefer them. Here are some examples generated from the transcript of a lecture on the novel.

Beyond the scope of literature became *beyond the scorpion of litigation.* This felt 'right' – the law can have a sting in its tail etc. The phrase slotted neatly into a story about an acrimonious divorce. Later I was amazed to learn that astrologically Scorpio rules the eighth house which, among other things, is concerned with law.

These narratives have one aspect in common. They are in principle verifiable became *These nations have one aspiration in communication. They are in prison vermicidal.* This is probably not usable as it stands, but could be developed in some way as a comment on the human condition.

I am dealing with a mistake or a fiction becomes *I am deathless with a mistress or a fiddle* – which went straight into a short story.

Many others – original sources forgotten – are filed in my writer's notebook: eg 'Fanaticism – a quiet glazed thuggery.' 'A slimy new maggot abroad.' 'Two simpering canines with a cephalopod curate between them.' 'A vaudeville of dailies reappearing on the polo marsh.'

Checklist

Discover new plots and new forms of expression by using:

- branching narratives
- an added complication
- the question game
- plot-generating computer programmes
- S + 7.

CASE STUDIES

Karen can't stop doing S + 7

Karen is so fascinated by S + 7 that she is doing little else in the way of writing at the moment. Whenever she hears a memorable phrase she wants to rush to the dictionary and see how it would work out. When a friend came to baby-sit they spent the evening doing S + 7 instead of Karen going out. She has heard that the fascination wears off after a while, and is wondering when this will happen.

David is pleased with his plot-generating programme

David looked at several plot programmes, and eventually chose one of the more sophisticated. The basic principle is similar to 'branching narratives', which he also likes, but the programme generates multiple possibilities with little effort on his part. He was a bit concerned about spending the money, but feels it has helped him to put his novel back on course when he had been floundering. He hopes to recoup the money through his writing.

Sheila finds her style is changing

Sheila has noticed a definite change in her style. She feels her characters are more rounded and her approach more subtle. She feels able to get inside the characters and tell their story as though it were her own. This seems to have happened partly because of the new techniques she has been trying, partly because of the producer's advice and partly because of the confidence his interest gave her.

9

Crafting

So far we have been exploring right-brain techniques mainly for the purpose of generating ideas and material. In the process, we have studied some aspects of crafting, mainly through drawing on internalised knowledge (eg focusing attention on the mechanics of speech production in Chapter 4, and studying our reactions to other writers' methods in Chapters 4 and 5).

This chapter deals specifically with crafting. In keeping with the approach of this book, it offers a right-brain perspective on the subject – **perspective** being the operative word. The right brain puts things together in a non-linear way. Activities like completing jig-saw puzzles, recognising faces and 'chunking' ideas are what it does best. Unfortunately, story-making is ultimately a linear process and this is where strongly right-brain oriented writers can come unstuck. Analysing, sorting, sequencing – the processes involved in shaping and styling a finished piece – are mainly left-brain activities. All writers, regardless of their hemisphere preference, need to master these in order to communicate effectively with their readers.

There are many excellent books which approach the craft of writing in a practical left-brain way (see Further Reading for recommended examples). Their advice can be invaluable, particularly for genre writers needing to master the fine points of particular formats. A very good way of encouraging a happy partnership between right- and left-brain functions is to use the approaches suggested in this chapter alongside those described in books with a more technical orientation. Eventually the two strands can be woven together – which brings us to the next section.

WEAVING

By the time you come to craft your finished piece, you will have assembled relevant material from a number of sources: writer's notebook, dream journal, timed writing, guided visualisation, tarot spreads etc. Some will relate to characters, some to places, some to particular objects and some to feelings, mood and atmosphere. Having selected and sorted what you need, the task of weaving it all together begins.

As you weave character, place and mood together, tune in constantly to see how these various elements are responding to each other. How does the character feel about that place? How does the setting respond to the presence of the character? Which of them is responsible for the mood – or is it reciprocal? What situation might arise from bringing this person to this place?

Try using each of the elements – character, place, objects, feelings, atmosphere – as symbols or metaphors for each other. How does this affect the dynamics?

How is the pace affected by the language you have chosen (see Chapter 4)? Is the pace right for the atmosphere or mood you are trying to convey? Is the language suited to the place and the character?

If the piece you are developing is part of a longer work, use the same interactive approach when weaving it into the main fabric. Dialogue with all the elements concerned. Treat the new piece as you would any newcomer to a group. Introduce it with tact and awareness.

- Make the weaving process itself the subject of timed writing.

PLOT SHAPING

With certain genres, for example standard screen-plays, sit-coms and twist-in-the-tale short stories, the basic shape is set and the task is to write to it. It is like being given a recipe and assembling the ingredients accordingly.

When not writing within a specific genre, we have choices about the form our work will finally take. To pursue the cooking metaphor, we look at the ingredients we have, and find or create a recipe which will make the best use of them. Many strongly right-brained writers are happier with this approach. However, just as a hastily improvised recipe can let you down, stories that are insufficiently planned can end up going nowhere.

Many creative people struggle with the idea of structure. It can conjure images of algebra, AGMs, tax forms and a thousand other things which render the muse dry-mouthed and dysfunctional. Novelist Alison Harding prefers to view structure as organic – an integral part of story-making, just as sentence construction is an integral part of meaning-making. As with the weaving process above, this shifts emphasis away from 'should' and 'ought', towards a more muser-friendly consideration of how the story *wants* and *needs* to be told.

With this approach, the story is acknowledged as a living entity. The structure evolves as a result of inner dialogue with characters, setting and plot. Details are checked out as if compiling a biography. 'Is this how it was? Have I emphasised that strongly enough? Is this the best way of telling it?'

There are numerous forms which our evolving plan might take.

Try out different designs

Organise your notes
A planning strategy used by a number of writers is that of putting ideas, scenes, descriptive passages etc on separate sheets of paper and shuffling them around until a workable pattern emerges. Some writers blu-tack these notes to the wall, some pin them to a board or lay them out on the floor.

Index cards are a more manageable option. Their size also encourages concise note-making. Several well-organised writer friends plan their work on index cards and file them, initially under topics and later under chapter headings. (Index trays long enough to accommodate a full-length play or novel are quite expensive. Shoe boxes are a viable alternative, and cost nothing.)

Some planning systems are suggested below.

Story boards
These are often used in planning screened drama. The sheet or board is divided into squares, one for each scene. In each square, everything the director or continuity person needs to know about that scene is noted either in words or sketches. The end result is like an expanded version of the narrative steps described in the last chapter, and provides a valuable overview which enables any repetitions or omissions to be corrected.

The method is equally useful to writers, both at the initial planning stage and as a means of keeping track of changes as the work progresses. Notes (on index cards) can be grouped on or around the appropriate squares. At the initial planning stage a story board for Little Red Riding Hood might look something like Figure 7.

Red Riding Hood sets out
Describe temperament,
appearance.
Describe scenery, weather
Atmosphere of wood
How is she feeling?
Actions en route?

Meeting with wolf
Wolf's appearance
Innocence/Guile – convey contrast
through body lang/dialogue

Wolf finds out where gran lives

Wolf eats grandmother
Sketch gran's appearance
Emphasise fear
Rapid conclusion

(Wolf remembers eating
younger humans, compares?)

Wolf dressed as gran tricks RRH
Innocence/Guile
Dialogue 'Oh Grandma what
big ears . . .'

Wolf eats RRH
Dramatic Climax
Shock (wolf's open jaws from
RRH's viewpoint?)
Sounds
Reader must believe evil has
triumphed.

Rescue by father
Briefly refer to father's
appearance – stress **action**.
Shock – to wolf (axe descending
from wolf's viewpoint?)
Father described from RRH's
viewpoint on emerging from wolf.
Comfort. Relief

Fig. 7. A story board for Little Red Riding Hood.

Happiness, innocence. Underlying unease	Unease confirmed	Mortal danger	Child in mortal danger	Dramatic climax	Rescue
Child in forest on sunny day alone	Threatening figure – troll, giant, witch wolf?	Evil figure attacks vulnerable person	Evil figure disguised	Child's terror	Adult appears – slays evil figure
Hint of danger	Innocence/Guile – convey contrast through body language/dialogue	Terror. Murder	Innocence/Guile	Horrific sounds	
Red garments – bloodshed?					Comfort. Relief
Where is child going?	Innocently reveals address of vulnerable person	Child now in danger	Child trusts evil figure	Evil triumphs	All is well
				Murder?	

Fig. 8.   Pictorial score adapted to story-making.

Pictorial score

Musician Penny Gordon plans her compositions by drawing a linear picture that outlines the moods she wishes to evoke in the piece. She uses colour, pattern, and a mixture of abstract and pictorial representation. Underneath each sector she sketches her ideas in words and music.

The pattern of moods in such a picture could be inspired by a painting, a piece of music, a poem, a specific event – anything which affects feeling and mood. For an example of how this mood-led strategy could be applied to story-making, see Figure 8. (and imagine the colours). This particular example shows how a story such as Red Riding Hood might have evolved from the ideas generated by such a mood-picture. Like the story board, it provides a valuable overview of work in progress – as do the next three approaches.

Route map

Map the route of your story as if it were the Central Line on the London Underground, each stop representing a narrative step in the main plot. Show any sub-plots as auxiliary lines. Group idea sheets or index cards around the appropriate stops.

Topographical map

This type of map shows the location of key events in a story. Tolkein's maps of Middle Earth and A A Milne/E H Shephard's map of Christopher Robin's world are well-known examples. Some other layouts on which a story could be based are: a meal set out on a table, the plans of a house or garden, a musical score, a seating plan, a photograph, a game board or games pitch.

Family tree

The longer the work, the more comprehensive the drawing up of family trees needs to be in order to prevent chronological errors. A family tree can also be the starting point around which the story is structured.

Flow chart

Often used in computing, a flow chart shows possible paths through a programme or task. The Yes/No choices which have to be negotiated in using a cashpoint machine could be plotted as a simple flow chart. Those involved in the self-assessment income tax forms would provide a far more elaborate example.

A flow chart can be used to chart a character's progress. Unlike narrative trees, which give two choices at each juncture, flow charts operate on an 'if this happens, do this' basis. Also unlike narrative trees, they can jump several steps forwards or backwards, return the user to the beginning or eject them from the system entirely. See Red Riding Hood flow chart (Figure 9).

Instructions, directions and other sources of information
Stories have been based on recipes, menus, knitting patterns, the weather forecast, the ten commandments and train timetables, to give but a few examples.

Storage bases
Anything in which items are gathered together and viewed as a collection can be used as the basis of a story. A chest of drawers, a china cabinet, a library, a fridge, a shed, a sewing box, all have their story to tell. Personal memories associated with the contents can be evoked through guided visualisation (as with the toy box and wardrobe in Chapter 6). Or the story of the objects and the events which brought them together can be told.

Tarot spread
There are many tarot spreads, both simple and complex, around which a story can be structured. Each position in the spread represents the answer to a question, so that the spread can be used as a plan with or without the accompanying cards. (See Figure 5 for an example.)

Inner workings
'Begin at the beginning', the King said, very gravely, 'and go on till you come to the end: then, stop.'
(Lewis Carroll: *Alice's Adventures in Wonderland*)

Within the basic structure of the plot there are, of course, many ways of telling the story, eg flash-back, implication, reported incident, symbolic representation, dream sequences, letters.

In *How to Write a Million*, Ansen Dibell says, 'All this structural hanky-panky isn't something to engage in just for the fun of it. Any departure from linear, sequential storytelling is going to make the story harder to read and call attention to the container rather than the content, the technique rather than the story those techniques should be serving.' She also

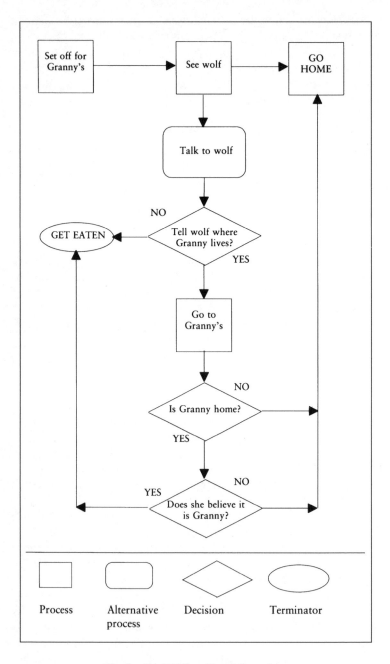

Fig. 9. Red Riding Hood flow chart.

advises, 'Make sure the running plot in your story's present is strong, clear and well established before splitting off to do *anything* else.'

However, even straight narrative is fraught with choice: past, present or future tense; first, second or third person – whose viewpoint? These are often difficult decisions to make. Try an inner dialogue with the elements in question. Study the effects achieved by other writers. Keep the following guidelines in mind:

- If it is difficult to decide between first and third person narrative, think about the basic temperament of the character. Are they introverted or extroverted, friendly or stand-offish? In other words, would they be happy to tell their own story, or would they rather somebody told it for them?

- Who is the audience? Would the character want to speak directly to them?

- If you choose present tense narrative, it is likely to quicken the pace. It is also very intimate. Are these the effects you want?

- Look again at the novel you studied in Chapters 4 and 5. Can any of the techniques used by that writer be adapted to your purposes?

- How will your current decisions affect your last line or last idea?

Write backwards
This is an approach used particularly when writing twist-in-the-tale stories and comedy sketches. In both instances the writer needs to set up certain expectations in the mind of the reader, viewer or listener in order to create the maximum surprise at the end. For this reason the ending is often worked out first and the rest of the story then 'written backwards' to a pre-determined structure.

The techniques used in both genres are very specific and require separate study if this is an avenue you wish to pursue (see Further Reading for further information). However, the idea of beginning with an ending and writing backwards from it can be applied to other types of story – as it was in Chapter 5. In that instance we brainstormed penultimate sentences, chose one, then created a new story by writing towards the new two-sentence ending.

This time we will work backwards step by step, first choosing a final sentence, then brainstorming scenarios which might have preceded it.

For example, some scenarios which might have preceded Ray Bradbury's final sentence 'Then . . . some idiot turned on the lights' are:

1. The boy opened the headmaster's drawer to return money stolen by his friend.

2. The men were standing naked in the middle of the women's changing room.

3. A film containing vital photographic evidence had just been removed from the camera.

4. The car's lights were wired to a bomb.

5. The woman thought the man in bed with her was her husband.

6. The funeral cortege was proceeding with dignity along the front at Blackpool.

Choose one brainstormed scenario, then one or more scenarios which could have preceded it. A scenario is then chosen to precede that and so on until the beginning of the story is reached. You then have a basic plot with which to work.

Checklist
When crafting work:

- blend right- and left-brain approaches

- tune in to various elements to see how they are responding to each other

- think of structure as organic

- choose an idea-organising system which gives you an overview

- check out other writers' solutions.

Also, if you want to write twist-in-the-tale stories or comedy sketches, you need to study the finer points involved in writing backwards.

FINE-TUNE YOUR CHARACTERS

- Study Chapters 2, 3 and 8 again. Use the exercises to get to know your characters even better.

- Use 10 × 10 as a safeguard against stereotyping.

- Study 'Focus on the words' and 'Focus on the sounds' (Chapter 4) again, to check that the language you have used to describe the characters really resonates with their particular personalities.

- Which actor or actress would you choose to play the part of your character? Imagine them in the role. Does this reveal any inconsistencies?

- Sit your character in an empty chair and talk to them. Change seats and reply as your character.

- Are there any questions you need to ask about your characters? Use the I Ching or Runes to help you find answers.

- If you have an astrology programme, look at the characters' natal charts again. Look at their house charts and transits. Use synastry (see Glossary) for further insight into their relationships.

- Choose a tarot spread to help you gain further insight.

NB If there are tarot cards you particularly enjoy working with, have them copied A4 size and laminated. This can be done quite cheaply at the large office supplies stores.

FINE-TUNE YOUR DIALOGUE

Check that every piece of dialogue you have written performs at least one of the following functions:

1. Conveys essential information.

2. Moves the story forward.

3. Reveals the character and mood of the person who is speaking.

4. Establishes the relationship between characters.

Although the mode of speech provides clues to a character's era, geographical origins and social class, dialogue alone should not be used to convey these.

Dialogue that does not perform any of the above four functions should be cut.

Skilfully handled dialogue can perform several of these functions at once. Work at making yours more economical in this respect.

Check also that the dialogue is distinctive – that only the person in question could have said those words. If any section still sounds like dummy dialogue – ie anyone could have said it – it needs fine-tuning.

INVENT A PURPOSE

If you have no specific purpose for the telling of your tale, invent one. Do you want to make a specific point, raise awareness, entertain, shock? Which particular sector of the public would you like to influence or affect? Having a specific purpose and a specific target audience in mind will help to focus your thoughts.

STYLE AND CLARITY

Does your work sometimes suffer from 'stylism'? Do verbosity, minimalism and originality lure you like sirens onto the rocks of mumbo-jumbo? Does your internal critic then sail past with a loud hailer, shouting comments about 'trying to be clever' – and does your novel subsequently end up at the back of a drawer for another few months? Head for the calmer waters of Chapter 2 and 'Tune in'. Inside is where your true writer's voice is to be found. Like structure, it is organic and cannot be bolted on.

Repeat some of the exercises from Chapter 2, then return to the piece you are crafting at the moment. The following exercise will improve both its style and its clarity.

Pare down

Imagine you have received details of a competition. The story you are in the process of finishing is just right for it – except that it is 500 words too long. Weed out the non-essentials until your story fits the required length.

Pare down again

Now write it again as a 1,000-word story. Again – a very useful exercise in crafting. This time you may lose some elements which deserve to be kept, but you will probably have made a number of unexpected improvements as well.

Select the best

Select the best elements of your two shortened stories and combine them to produce a final prizeworthy draft.

Checklist

- Use a variety of methods to get to know your characters thoroughly.

- Pay particular attention to the way they express themselves verbally.

- Focus your thoughts by inventing a purpose for your story.

- Reduce the number of words you have used to tell it.

- Reduce them again.

CASE STUDIES

Karen comes out writing backwards

Karen has emerged from her S + 7 phase with what she describes as a 'warped imagination'. Just the idea of 'writing backwards' has enormous appeal, and she is exploring it in various ways. She thinks the notice-board at work would make a good starting point for a short story, with dialogue based on people's comments as they read it.

David gets a kick out of paring down

David hates what he calls 'flowery writing', with long sentences and a great deal of description. He likes the idea of making his prose as sparse as possible, particularly the dialogue. He is also thinking of structuring his novel along the lines of a weekly profit and loss return, kept by a detective to record the successes and failures of his cases.

Sheila finds an organic approach interesting

Sheila is writing a play for the local youth theatre group. The group has been exploring the theme 'man's inhumanity'. Much of the material in the play has evolved from improvisation, and this is teaching Sheila a lot about dialogue. The speeches are generally much shorter than she has been used to writing, and this is having a marked influence on the style.

10

Editing

APPRECIATING THE LEFT BRAIN

As discussed in previous chapters, the right brain puts things together in a non-linear way. Its knowledge is gained through images rather than words. It can process many kinds of information simultaneously and can make great leaps of insight. It understands metaphor, creates dreams and fantasies, wonders 'What if . . . ?' Such abilities generally receive less encouragement in the worlds of school and work than those which the left brain offers, eg logic, mathematical precision, ability to label accurately, order, neatness. One of the main aims of this book is to redress that particular balance.

However, this is not to suggest that the right brain is superior to the left brain. On the contrary, they complement each other in most activities. In fact after the age of five when specialisation of the hemispheres is complete, one cannot function efficiently without the other. A writer certainly could not function without access to the specialist activities of the left brain. It controls speech, reading, and writing. It recalls information and knows how to spell. As discussed in Chapter 9, the essential crafting and editing skills of analysing, sorting, selecting and sequencing are mainly left-brain activities.

Harmonising the hemispheres

The ideal is to get the two sides of the brain working in harmony, each supporting the other, doing what it does best while not getting in the other's way. The dynamics of your particular left-brain/right-brain partnership can be observed by returning to the hand exploration exercise in Chapter 2. How did the two hands react to each other when you first did it?

- Try the exercise again. Compare the results. Does either side of the partnership need encouragement? Is some negotiation needed? How do you feel about each side? Does your attitude need some adjustment?

A good working relationship between both hemispheres, will make the strongly left-brain task of editing less daunting. Although the two hemispheres work together on most activities, their way of processing information differs. The extent to which they are involved at a given time depends on the particular task. Peter Vincent says that experience has taught him never to write and edit at the same sitting. When he starts work on a script he lets the ideas, however off-the-wall, flow from his right brain unimpeded. 'Anything can seem funny at this stage,' he says. At the end of several days' writing he welcomes the good sense of his left brain, which steps in to sort out what will or will not work.

Confident handing over of the helm to the left brain in this way requires the services of a supportive rather than a censorious internal critic.

BEFRIEND YOUR CRITIC

In *The Creative Fire*, Clarissa Pinkola Estes uses the story of the brave dog Gelert as a metaphor for the misguided critical process. Gelert, the King's favourite dog, is found covered in blood beside the upturned cradle of the baby prince. Thinking the dog has slain the child, the king kills him. He then finds the child unharmed beneath the cradle, next to the body of the wolf from which Gelert saved him.

The wolf and the dog can be seen as aspects of our internal critic: the wolf a murderous aspect that wants to destroy the products of our creativity, the dog an ally, who wants to serve us and our creations.

Trauma, conditioning and poor judgement can lead us to mistrust the dog and side with the wolf. Successful editing requires us to believe in the dog and to tame the wolf so that its power is harnessed for our purposes. As with the left and right brain, we can then develop a productive working partnership. The ultimate aim is to integrate and work with all aspects of ourselves in this way.

A good starting point is to get to know both sides of the critic better through guided visualisation. This will work best if done in relation to a current piece of work which is at the editing stage.

Guided visualisation – get to know your internal critic
Close your eyes and focus on a current piece of writing.
Which parts of it please you? Which parts of it are giving
you trouble? What difficulties are you experiencing? Be as
specific as possible.
Allow an image of your helpful internal critic to come to
mind. When you have a clear image, give it a name.
What sort of voice does your helpful critic have? What sort of
things does this critic normally say? How do you feel about
this?
Ask this critic to say what they think about your current
work. What do they think about the parts you like? What
advice can they offer about your difficulties?
Allow this image to fade. Allow an image of your negative
critic to come to mind.
When you have a clear image, give this negative critic a
name.
What is this critic's voice like? What sort of things does this
critic normally say?
How do you feel about this?
Ask this critic to comment on your current work – its good
points and bad points.
Has this critic got any advice to offer?
Allow this image to fade now, and spend some time reflecting
on the experience.
Which critic are you more inclined to believe? Which one do
you like best?
Which do you find more helpful? Will you act on the advice
given by either?
In a few moments you are going to bring these two critics
together. Is this likely to cause a problem? If so, you could
call on the mediating skills of a talisman, tarot character or
other helper.
Allow these two critics to meet each other now. Encourage
each to say what they see as each other's good and bad
points. What concessions are they prepared to make in order
to be able to work together?
Ask the two critics to discuss your current work. What
changes would each one make? What arguments does each

give regarding the other's changes? Allow plenty of time for this discussion to develop. Intervene and comment as needed. Before you draw this discussion to a close, ask each of the critics what they need from you in order to be able to work in partnership.

Thank them both for their help, return and make any notes you need to make.

Checklist

- Right-brain thinking is not superior to left-brain thinking. It is just different. We need to be aware of the specific skills of each side.

- Right brain and left brain work in partnership. We need to enable this process by recognising the contribution of each one.

- Our critic can be very useful at the editing stage. Fostering its positive aspects will make this process more productive.

PLAY THE EDITING GAME

The suggestion that editing can be approached as a game is made partly to reduce anxiety in strongly right-brained writers, and partly to draw attention to the capricious nature of editing requirements. Unless you are in the position of being able to follow Polonius' dictate, 'This above all: to thine own self be true,' editing criteria will vary according to market, genre, and current taste. One editor will like your style but not your story line, another the reverse. For one magazine your story is too long, for another too short, for another it is just right, but the heroine is too old – and so on.

Below are listed ten aspects of your work which will require scrutiny whatever your current criteria. Some general questions are asked under each aspect. As a focusing exercise, make this into an 'Editing 10 × 10' by adding more questions to suit your particular requirements.

1. The beginning

- Does it really grab the reader's attention? (If not, you could lose your audience altogether.)

- Does it intrigue, shock, strike a chord, plunge the reader straight into the action? (See Chapter 5.)

- Does it make you want to read on?

- Is the 'implicit contract' it makes with the reader a valid one? (See Chapter 5.)

- Have you read the beginning aloud to anyone and asked for their feedback?

2. Characters

- Have you brought them to life? Will the readers feel they know these people and will they care what happens to them? (See Chapters 2, 4 and 6.)

- Are your characters authentic? Do their descriptions 'ring true'? Are clothes, speech patterns and cultural references right for the period and location?

- Is their behaviour consistent with their personalities? Is their appearance consistent? In longer works, continuity of costume and hair colour/style may need to be checked. A story board is helpful in this respect (see Chapter 9).

- Do any elements of your characterisation need more emphasis? Have you asked anyone for feedback about this?

3. Setting

- Have you given the reader a clear picture of the surroundings?

- Have you done your research thoroughly? Are clothing, architecture, artefacts, cultural references in keeping with the historical period?

- Have you checked continuity in this respect? Again, a story board can be useful for this purpose.

- Have you conveyed the atmosphere you intended to convey?

4. Plot

- Is the story line absolutely clear?

- Could it be set out in narrative steps as in Chapter 8 or could you plot it on a route map, as in Chapter 9?

- Were any 'added complications' fruitful, or were they side-tracks which diverted attention from the main thrust of the story? In the example given, Cinderella languishes in a dungeon while the prince, ignorant of her plight, is far away fighting. The reader has the overview, which creates dramatic tension. This path has many possibilities, eg 'Having received no word from the beautiful stranger, the prince concludes she does not care for him. Eschewing love, he agrees to a politically sound marriage with a princess from a neighbouring kingdom. As the day of the marriage draws near, Cinderella tries to send the glass slipper to him but the ugly sisters intercept it.' This all adds to the story's emotional impact.

  If the Prince had gone off to war and Cinderella had gone home and worried about him for a year or so, this would be a side-track. Other than a chance to reveal the strength of Cinderella's love, it would serve no dramatic function. In fact it would confuse the plot and destroy the story's momentum.

5. Story-telling vehicles

- Have you chosen the best way to tell your story?

- Have you used straight narrative throughout, or have you interspersed this with flash-back, dream sequences, letters and other devices? What were the reasons for these choices? (See Chapter 9.)

- What tense have you chosen and whose viewpoint have you used? Do you have sound reasons for these choices? Might other choices be more effective?

- Have you used dialogue as a story-telling vehicle? What were your reasons for doing so? Was it always a good choice? (See Chapter 9.)

6. Dialogue

- Is your dialogue realistic?

- Is it authentic?

- Is your dialogue consistent with the characters' historical period, geographical origins, and social class?

- Is it distinctive? Could only that character have made that particular speech?

- Have you read your dialogue aloud? How does it sound?

- Have you checked that every piece of dialogue you have written performs at least one of the following functions:

  - conveys essential information
  - moves the story forward
  - reveals the character and mood of the person who is speaking
  - establishes the relationship between characters.

7. Feelings

'Proper structure occurs when the right things happen at the right time to create maximum emotion.'

(Michael Hauge: *Writing Screenplays that Sell*)

It is also important to remember that these 'right things' must happen to *people* and that these must be people about whom the audience cares. *Casualty* is watched avidly by millions, not because it is about a hospital but because it is about people in crisis.

- How heart-rending or heart-warming is your story?

- Could your characterisation benefit from some fine-tuning to help the audience care a little more?

- Are the 'right things happening at the right time' – or are changes needed?

8. Pace

- Do any passages interfere with the pace you intended? Have you read any doubtful passages aloud?

- Have you checked sentence length, use of punctuation, use of active or passive voice and of present participles?

- Have you checked the number of images and their speed of presentation?

- Have you checked the length of sounds involved in speaking the words? (See Chapter 4.)

9. Style

'You don't have to consciously cultivate a style. Just learn to write well and your style will emerge . . . If you peer too closely at your style you will end up parodying yourself. Your writing voice must flow from you naturally, just as your conversational voice does.'

(Gary Provost: *Make Your Words Work*)

- Have you 'tuned in', as suggested in Chapter 9? Returning to the exercises in Chapter 2 before dealing with any 'iffy' passages will pay great dividends.

- Are there any elements of 'stylism'? Does style sometimes take precedence over clarity? (See Chapter 9.) Describe your style.

- Have you used too many adjectives? Have you used too few?

- Have you engaged in any stylistic 'hanky-panky . . . just for the fun of it?' (See Chapter 9.) If so – was it fun?

10. The end

- How effective is it?

- Is it satisfying – or does it leave the reader feeling stranded and/or disappointed?

- Is it active or reflective?

- Is there a link with the beginning, which brings the story full circle?

- Does it round the story off, make you cry, make you shudder?

- Can you improve it? (See Chapter 5.)

CASE STUDIES

Karen needs the discipline

Karen dreads editing and puts it off for as long as possible. However, when she does get round to it she is invariably pleased with the results. A clear story line and an effective ending are aspects of her work which usually need attention. She often starts with a good idea and a great opening sentence and then peters out or gets side-tracked. She realises her approach can be undisciplined, and she is going to make an effort to spend more time planning her work in future.

David really enjoys editing

Editing is one of David's favourite occupations. At work he used to be proud of his concise reports. He now enjoys using the same skills in his fiction writing. He has finished the first draft of his novel (having abandoned the idea of keeping a profit and loss record as structure, but retained it as an idiosyncrasy of his main character). Ironically, he planned his work so thoroughly that very little editing is necessary.

Sheila is successful with both her plays

After much editing and rewriting – particularly of dialogue – Sheila's youth play has been performed to much local acclaim. While still on a high from this success, she received a phone call from the radio producer who had expressed an interest in her play. He was pleased with the alterations she made and wants to produce the play next season. Sheila is delighted that her hard work and perseverance have finally paid off.

Glossary

Astrocartography. A branch of astrology which advises on choices of location.

Alchemy. Medieval forerunner of chemistry, particularly concerned with the transmutation of base metals into gold or silver. Symbolically a process of transformation.

Archetypes. Ancient images arising from fundamental human experiences. The basic stuff of myths and legends, manifest in universally recognisable roles or concepts, eg mother, child, revenge, old age.

Aromatherapy. Balancing of mental and physical energies through the use of essential oils from plants, usually inhaled or applied in diluted form to the skin.

Astrology. The study of the planets in our solar system and the way their energies and movements are reflected in our lives and characters.

Bioenergetics. A body-focused psychotherapy developed by Dr Alexander Lowen which aims to integrate body and mind.

Brainwave alteration. Brainwave frequencies are divided into four bands or 'states': **Beta** – highly alert, **Alpha** – calmly alert, **Theta** – hypnogogic or meditative, **Delta** – asleep. Brainwaves can be altered to produce these states through relaxation techniques, meditation and pulsing light or sound products designed for the purpose.

Chunking text. Grouping ideas around the page and outlining them, rather than recording them in a linear fashion. This aids both access and memory.

Circadian rhythms. (From the Latin: *circa die* – about a day). Metabolic rhythms found in most organisms, which generally coincide with the 24-hour day. Additional cycles related to attention span and sleep patterns have been observed in humans.

Decumbiture. An ancient astrological art used by physicians and herbalists to determine the best remedies to prescribe.

De-roling. Performing a series of grounding activities after guided visualisation or role-play in order to re-establish a sense of identity.

Gestalt therapy. A non-interpretative psychotherapy which aims to improve contact with the self and the environment by emphasising awareness.

Guided visualisation. An inner journey guided by scripted instructions.

Horary astrology. A branch of astrology which seeks to answer a specific question by consulting the chart of the moment when the question was asked.

I Ching. An ancient Chinese divination system which draws on the user's inner wisdom for help in solving problems. Coins are thrown and a hexagram formed. Every hexagram is associated with an 'answer' in the form of a riddle.

Internal critic. An inner voice which can cause self-doubt and diminish confidence.

Lucid dream. A dream which the dreamer recognises as such and can therefore influence the outcome.

Psyche. Innermost being, essential self, soul, spirit.

Psychotherapy. Sometimes referred to as 'talking therapy'. The non-invasive treatment of neurotic and stress-related disorders through therapeutic relationship with a qualified practitioner.

Repetitive stress syndrome. Physical disorder brought about by repeated use of one body part eg housemaid's knee, tennis elbow. Writers may develop symptoms in wrists, hands and eyes.

Right/left brain. Each side of the brain has its own specialised functions and processes information in its own way. The left side works through logic, the right through intuition. Although they work together for most activities, one side will dominate according to the task.

Runes. An Ancient Norse divination system by which marked stones are drawn singly or in spreads in order to gain insight into a difficulty.

S + 7. A technique developed by a group of French experimental novelists. ('S' may stand for *sujet*). A text is selected and its nouns, verbs and adjectives replaced by words which appear seven places away from them in a dictionary.

Shadow self. A person's hidden side, of which they are unaware. Dark in the sense of 'mysterious'. Not necessarily disturbing, but possessing qualities not normally displayed by that person.

Stylism. Pursuit of style at the expense of authenticity and clarity.

Subconscious. The part of the mind which operates below the level of full consciousness.

Synastry. A branch of astrology which compares the chart of two individuals to discover the strengths and weaknesses of their relationship.

Tarot. A system of 78 cards depicting archetypal characters and experiences, it is the forerunner of modern playing cards, and dates at least from medieval times. Because the mystic symbolism of the tarot makes it an ideal tool for personal growth, it has been adapted to the mythology of many different traditions.

10 × 10. A grid used as the basis for brainstorming 100 'facts' about a given character.

Timed writing. Writing to a preset time without stopping, crossing out or thinking. Used as a warm-up exercise and to by-pass the internal critic.

Tuning in. Becoming still, focusing on a particular issue, and seeking answers in a meditative way.

Word honeycomb. A word association technique starting with 16 words and moving towards a single word in the centre.

Word web. A word association technique which moves outwards from one central word.

Writing backwards. A technique used by writers when it is necessary to set up certain expectations in the reader's mind, eg in crime writing, twist-in-the-tale stories and comedy.

Further Reading

ASTROLOGY

Basic
Understanding Astrology, Sasha Fenton (Thorsons).
Parker's Astrology, Julia and Derek Parker (Dorling Kindersley).
Astrology, a Cosmic Science, Isabel M Hickey (CRCS Publications).
Mythic Astrology, Ariel Guttman and Kenneth Johnson (Llewellyn Publications).

Specialised
Horary Astrology, Dr Marc Edmund Jones (Aurora Press).
Relating, Liz Greene (Thorsons).
The Development of the Personality, Liz Greene and Howard Sasportas (Penguin).
Synastry, Ronald Davison (Aurora Press).

DREAMWORK

Dream Sharing, Robin Shohet (Crucible).
Lucid Dreaming, Stephen LaBerge and Howard Rheingold (Ballantine Books).
What Your Dreams Can Teach You, Alex Lukeman (Llewellyn Publications).

GENERAL REFERENCE

A Dictionary of Symbols, Tom Chetwynd (Paladin).
The Oxford Companion to the Mind, ed Richard L. Gregory (OUP).
Consciousness Explained, Daniel C Dennett (The Penguin Press).
The Elements of the I Ching, Stephen Karcher (Element Books).
Tarot for Beginners, Kristyna Arcati (Hodder and Stoughton).

VISUALISATION

At a Journal Workshop, Ira Progoff (Tarcher, Putnam).
Awareness, John O Stevens (Eden Grove).
Life Choices & Life Changes Through Imagework, Diana Glouberman (Unwin).
Walking Through Walls, Will Parfitt (Element Books).
What We May Be, Piero Ferrucci (Turnstone Press).

WRITING

Becoming a Writer, Dorothea Brande (Macmillan).
Comedy Writing Secrets, Melvin Helitzer (Writer's Digest Books).
The Craft of Writing Poetry, Alison Chisolm (Allison and Busby).
Creating a Twist in the Tale, Adèle Ramet (How To Books).
Fast Fiction, Roberta Allen (Story Press).
How to Write Comedy, Brad Ashton (Elm Tree Books).
The Art of Fiction, David Lodge (Penguin).
Twenty Master Plots and How to Build Them, Ronald B Tobias (Piatkus).
Word Power, Julian Birkett (A & C Black).
Write for Life, Nicki Jackowska (Element).
Write for Publication, Chriss McCallum (How To Books).
Writing Past Dark, Bonnie Friedman (Harper Perennial).
Zen in the Art of Writing, Ray Bradbury (Joshua Odell).

References

NON-FICTION BOOKS

The Right-Brain Experience, Marilee Zedenek, (Corgi).
Writing Down the Bones, Natalie Goldberg, (Shambala).
Wild Mind, Natalie Goldberg, (Rider).
Morning Contemplation, Osho, (Boxtree).
Not a Sentimental Journey, Ed. Jo Davis, (Gunbyfield Publishing).
A Writer's Notebook, (Exley Publications).
Dreams, Carl Jung, (Ark Paperbacks).
Dreams and Destiny, (Marshall Cavendish).
The Interpretation of Dreams, Sigmund Freud, (Penguin).
The Elements of Dreamwork, Strephon Kaplan-Williams, (Element Books).
The Dream Lover, Les Peto (Quantum).
Gestalt Counselling in Action, Petruska Clarkson, (Sage).
Writing Screenplays that Sell, Michael Hauge, (Elm Tree Books).
Make Your Words Work, Gary Provost, (Writer's Digest Books).
How to Write a Million, Dibell, Scott Card and Turco, (Robinson Publishing).

FICTION

The Waves, Virginia Woolf, (Hogarth Press).
Orlando, Virginia Woolf, (Virago).
To the Lighthouse, Virginia Woolf, (Virago).
Cat's Eye, Margaret Atwood, (Virago).
Republic of Love, Carol Shields, (Flamingo).
Dinner at the Homesick Restaurant, Anne Tyler, (QPD Edition).
If on a winter's night a traveller, Italo Calvino, (Picador).
The Count of Monte Cristo in *Time and the Hunter*, Italo Calvino, (Abacus).
This Way for the Gas, Ladies and Gentlemen, Tadeusz Borowski, (Penguin).
Behind the Scenes at the Museum, Kate Atkinson, (Black Swan).

Still, Adam Thorpe, (QPD Edition).
The October Game in *Long After Midnight*, Ray Bradbury, (Grafton).
Hotel du Lac, Anita Brookner, (Jonathan Cape).
Ride the Iron Horse, Majorie Darke.
Dr Jekyll and Mr Hyde, Robert Louis Stevenson.
Lord of the Rings, J. R. R. Tolkein, (Unwin).
The World of Pooh, A. A. Milne, (Methuen).
Alice's Adventures in Wonderland, Lewis Carroll.

TAROT PACKS

The Arthurian Tarot, Caitlin and John Matthews. Illustrator; Miranda Gray, (Thorsons).
The Mythic Tarot, Juliet Sharman-Burke and Liz Greene. Illustrator: Tricia Newell, (Rider).
The Osho-Zen Tarot, Osho. Commentary/Illustr; Ma Deva Padma, (St Martin's Press).

TAPES

The Creative Fire, Clarissa Pinkola Estes (Sounds True).

PERSONAL COMMENTS

Marjorie Darke
Jo Davis
Diane Gittins
Alison Harding
Les Peto
Peter Vincent

Useful Addresses

ASTROLOGICAL SOFTWARE

Astrocalc UK, 67 Peascroft Road, Hemel Hempstead, Herts HP3 8ER.

Roy Gillett Consultants, 32 Glynswood, Camberley, Surrey GU15 1HU.

Midheaven Bookshop, 396 Caledonian Road, London N1 1DN.

World of Wisdom, 20 Potters Lane, New Barnet, Herts EN5 5BH.

ASTROLOGY CORRESPONDENCE COURSES

The English Huber School, PO Box 118, Knutsford, Cheshire WA16 8TG.

The Mayo School, Alvana Gardens, Tregavethan, Truro, Cornwall TR4 9EN.

PERSONAL GROWTH PRODUCTS AND INFORMATION

LifeTools, Freepost SK 1852, Macclesfield SK10 2YE.

New World Music Ltd, Freepost ANG 441, The Barn, Beccles, Suffolk NR34 8BR.

Osho Purnima Distribution, Greenwise, Vange Park Rd, Basildon, Essex SS16 5LA.

Rontronics, 96 Dartmouth Park Hill, London N19 5HU.

SCRIPTS

Book City, 308 N. San Fernando Blvd, Dept 101, Burbank CA 91502 USA.

Faber and Faber Ltd, 3 Queen Square, London WC1N 3AU.

TAPES

BBC Radio, Broadcasting House, London W1A 1AA.
Sounds True, 735 Walnut Street, Colorado 80302, USA.

WRITERS' SOFTWARE

Dreampack for Writers (Shareware), www.dreampack.com
Money Flow Promotions, 16 Link House, Leat Street, Tiverton,
   Devon EX16 5LJ.
Plots Unlimited, www.ashleywilde.com
ScriptWorks, 111 Queens Crescent, London NW5 4EY.

WRITERS' WEBSITES

The Writers' Internet Resource Guide, www.novalearn.com/wirg

Index